IF ONLY I COULD believe!

IF ONLY I COULD believe!

Wim Rietkerk

solway

First published in the UK 1997 by Solway

03 02 01 00 99 98 97   7 6 5 4 3 2 1

Solway is an imprint of Paternoster Publishing,
P.O. Box 300, Carlisle, Cumbria CA3 0QS UK

Verses of hymns or choruses are quoted from *Mission Praise*
(London: Marshall Pickering, 1990)

Translated from the Dutch edition *Ik wou dat ik kòn geloven*
(Kampen: Kok Voorhoeve, 1993)

British Library Cataloguing in Publication Data

A catalogue record for this book
is available from the British Library.

ISBN 1–900507–36–6

Typeset by Photoprint, Torquay, Devon
Printed in the U.K. by Mackays of Chatham PLC, Kent

Contents

Preface

First my deep thanks to all who have been involved in bringing this book to life. During the Middle Ages it often happened that authors and poets would not put their name to their work — behind it lay the idea that such a work originated from 'us all, together'. That is how I also experienced writing this book. Most chapters started life as lectures. Then someone typed it, another corrected and edited it, and I added new perspectives which evolved during discussions after the lecture. The idea for a book finally made sense when so many people 'found it helpful'. So I claim nothing more than to share here with you who have not been able to join our lecture evenings at L'Abri that which I have learnt as a result of many discussions.

This book is written both for those who have stood on the threshhold of faith but then found it impossible to step across and for those who have entered the faith but have subsequently felt themselves again riddled with doubts and unbelief. It is for those who want to believe but find they cannot — for believers who sometimes feel deeply unbelieving, as well as for unbelievers who sometimes feel a deep longing to believe.

Many stumbling blocks can obstruct or trip up a robust faith. In this book I will concentrate on emotional stumbling blocks such as experiencing difficulty in trust, disappointment, confused feelings of guilt and shame, fear and anxiety, bereavement, the challenges of our particular stage of life, and confused notions of personal identity. I have included insights I gained from my studies in pastoral psychology at the University of Utrecht and also those useful insights from contemporary humanists like Erikson and Riemann which complement and expand a biblical understanding of life.

I have written with both individual and group study in mind — thinking especially of students in education and the caring professions (who need much discernment in their courses in psychology, psychotherapy and pastoral counselling in order to extract the kernels of truth and helpful common sense from their humanistic resources). For their benefit I have included a summary at the end of every chapter, questions for discussion, related Bible readings and a list of books for further reading. I encourage those who read *If only I could believe!* on their own to keep a notebook or diary, to honestly answer the questions at the end of each section and to discuss what they have learned with a friend who knows them well.

About L'Abri

L'Abri started in *Switzerland* in the fifties when Francis and Edith Schaeffer opened their home to 'shelter' young people struggling with intellectual questions about the meaning of life and the existence of God. Several L'Abri centres now exist where Christian families live in community to provide a shelter for anyone needing 'time out' to seek honest answers to honest questions, traumatic or persistent. At L'Abri students follow a personal and individually guided study programme, but the emphasis is on 'community' and at least as much learning takes place in conversation during meal times, or in struggling with the daily share of manual chores, as in the study room. Occasional lectures, the enjoying and discussing of films, art and music, games, Bible studies and prayer times are all part of the innovative, 'whole-life' L'Abri tradition pioneered by the Schaeffers.

The *Dutch branch* of L'Abri consists of a home hosting weekly lectures and an 'open' study room in the heart of historic Utrecht. Alternatively students can join weekend programmes or stay for longer residential periods at the country house, Kortenhoeve, near Eck-en-Wiel.

The *English branch* of L'Abri is situated in the village of Greatham, about 50 miles southwest of London, and functions as a fully residential study centre. Prospective students are best advised to book in advance. Other branches or study groups operate in *Korea, Sweden, USA, Australia* and *India*. For further information, write to:

- L'Abri, Chalet Bellevue, 1884 Huemoz, Switzerland, or
- L'Abri, Kromme Nieuwe Gracht 90, 3512 HM Utrecht, Netherlands, or
- L'Abri, The Manor House, Greatham, Liss, Hants, GU33 6HF, UK.

Introduction: If only I could believe!

It was the spring of 1984. My wife and I had been invited to the home of a lady whose children had attended a conference with us. She did not see herself as a believer but wanted to talk about life. We talked for a long time and touched on deep things such as the existence of God alongside so much suffering in the world, and whether or not faith is a kind of subconscious wish-fulfilment. She explained also how she had come to discard the religious upbringing of her childhood. As the conversation became more personal it soon became clear that the intellectual questions surrounding the existence of God were not really worrying her. 'If only I could believe!' she finally exclaimed. However much we tried, our discussion got no further that day.

Many people would recognize themselves in her exclamation — 'If only I could believe!' Or they would remember a discussion which took a similar turn and which invariably ended there. For if we are honest we have no reply to such a confession. It is a stalemate. It is pointless to stack up more arguments for the faith, except to hide behind them. It is a very different situation to one where a person had never heard about God or has a deep resistance to God with clear and solid prejudices against the faith.

In this book I want to break through such a stalemate. It is my deep conviction that we can achieve such a goal; and we *have* to — for the marvellous thing is that when we do, we all gain. In the end, what makes it impossible for one person to come to faith is the same obstacle that makes it impossible for another person to grow in faith. Not just beginning to believe is blocked in this way, but also continuing to believe. So this book is equally applicable to believers who feel deeply unbelieving as to unbelievers who feel a deep longing to believe.

What is Faith?

Faith is trust. When we find it difficult to trust another person, we also find it difficult to put our trust in God. That is my starting point in this introductory chapter. Of course faith is more than trust. It is also knowledge — knowledge of a certain kind. In Hebrews 11:1 we read, 'Faith is being sure of what we hope for and certain of what we do not see.' Faith has to do with a reality which exists outside myself. It is there. But I cannot see it. It is only through revelation that I come into contact with true reality. I have to trust that it is there. And the way by which I become sure of the reality which I cannot see, is called faith.

Faith, then, has two aspects to it: knowing the truth, and trusting the person who told you the truth. The two

aspects are interrelated. It is beautifully illustrated by the
two words the Bible uses for truth. In the New Testament
the original Greek word for truth, *aletheia*, literally means
'unveiled reality'. It emphasizes objectivity and knowledge. But in the Old Testament the original Hebrew
word for truth, *emet*, literally means 'reality which gives us
solid ground under our feet'. It emphasizes the personal
relationship — as if the Hebrew writer wanted to say, 'You
will never know what is trustworthy if you have not
experienced how solid it is.' Put your feet on it! That is
trust. It reminds me of skating on a frozen lake. I might
well have heard that the ice was thick enough to skate on,
but it is only as I venture out and put my weight on it that
I will truly know how safe it is! This act of 'putting my
weight on it' is faith. Despite the message today that one
can never be sure of anything, the letter to the Hebrews
says that there is a way — faith — by which I can become
sure of the reality that is.

Being persuaded

Faith is trust. Trust is a matter of heart and emotions. But
trust is not an automatic human reaction and certainly not
in our day. 'It is a living thing,' Luther said, and even in
Bible times people have struggled with it. I think, for
example, of the prophet Jeremiah. After a period of deep
emotional stuggle, he exclaims: 'Oh Lord, you persuaded
me, and I was persuaded; you overpowered me and
prevailed' (Je. 20:7).

Here Jeremiah gives a personal testimony of how he
tried to evade the truth of God but had to submit when

God 'overpowered' him. The heading to this paragraph in the Old Testament is 'Jeremiah's complaint'. It is a personal testimony of how he tried all sorts of ways to escape the truth of God. But it closed in on him and finally he had to yield — 'You overpowered me and prevailed.' So Jeremiah expresses his faith, not as the result of abstract reasoning or careful calculation. No, much more alive, as the outcome of having wrestled with deep resistances that lived inside himself and having struggled to understand that which seemed, at first, incomprehensible. It was a *victory* over his own fears, but also a *surrendering* of himself to the truth. Assurance of faith comes from having been persuaded. And that brings me close to one of my goals with this book — to persuade *you* by stimulating you in that personal, all-determining battle to find the truth in person, despite crippling, deep, and often subconscious resistances.

In the case of Jeremiah, these resistances were intellectual and emotional. He had nagging intellectual questions (Je.14:9-19), but he had also deep emotional barriers (Je. 20:14-18). God spoke to both.

Being human involves more than reason and will

It would be painful to limit our questions and doubts only to that which relates to the intellect. Emotional barriers can be even more daunting to overcome. Similarly it is wrong to assume that an inability to believe is always caused by unwillingness. In fact, many people today are eager, searching, and willing to sacrifice in order to find certainty.

Much has been written and published by believers to deal with the intellectual questions regarding faith. That is excellent and important. And believers have often stressed the sinful unwillingness of human beings to bow before God's sovereignty. Rightly so. But why has the emotional side of our inability to come to faith been overlooked for so long? It is an area which is at least equally important.

One may think of the human personality as consisting of three components: the mind, the will, and the emotions. In this book I will defend the oneness of personal being. I will show that many *intellectual* questions result from *emotional* barriers (Ch. 2, 3); that many *emotional* problems are rooted in *intellectual* misunderstandings (Ch. 6); and that individual *choice and will* is important in the *emotional* make-up of personal being (Ch. 8).

Reason, will and emotion should be integrated. In our culture they are often split, divided. But in the process of coming to believe and growing in faith we can flounder when the emotional side of personal being is neglected — and that is why it is important to focus on this much neglected aspect at the present moment of time.

Pascal

I want to build on some of the ideas of Blaise Pascal (1623–62) who challenged Enlightenment thinking when he suggested that the real decisions about God and life are not made on the basis of reason alone. His most famous words are: 'The heart has its reasons that Reason does not know.'

'Reason's last step is the recognition that there are an infinite number of things which are beyond it. It is merely feeble if it does not go as far as to realize that' (*Pensées*, p.85). Pascal also recounts a long discussion with a sceptic. When the sceptic has rejected all the rational arguments for Christianity, Pascal moves a step further. He does not stop where rational arguments stop; on the contrary, he suggests that if these arguments cannot persuade the sceptic he might be hindered by his *passions*: 'If you are unable to believe, it is . . .because of your passions. . . . You will not be convinced by multiplying the proofs of God's existence but by diminishing your passions' (ibid. p.152)! The 'passions' Pascal talks about operate on two levels — that of the emotions and that of the will. Sceptics are afraid to lose their self-control; or they are too proud to be humiliated. Pascal's advice is simple: 'Act *as if* you believe, then your heart will follow!'

I do not know whether such an answer will satisfy those around us today. But it is true that sometimes it helps to act *as if*. It happened to the princess in the fairytale, 'Beauty and the Beast': when she kissed the monster *as if* it was a beautiful prince that is exactly what it appeared to be! At the moment she forced herself into obedience, submitting to that for which she had no natural sympathy, that which she most longed for, happened. Sometimes this is profound advice. Bend your will! Give in! Just do it! Even if you do not feel like it at all. But would it not be so much better also to feel like it?

Which brings me to consider the whole area of how we handle those emotional barriers which bar us from coming to faith. I will do this in the context of a brief outline of Christian apologetics since the Second World War.

a) Three steps

During the forties and fifties modern apologetics went through an 'intellectual phase' — and this continues to be a very meaningful aspect of the dialogue between Christians and humanists.

The Dutch philosopher Dr H. Dooyeweerd (1894–1977), in developing his Calvinistic Philosophy, held that 'If there is to be a real dialogue between Christians and non-Christians then it will have to deal with the underlying convictions (that each nourish) concerning reality' (in *Roots of Western Culture*, p.6). 'If the post-War dialogue is to contribute to the spiritual renewal of our nation, it must penetrate to that depth-dimension of human life where a person can no longer escape himself.' He analysed the 'ground motives' underlying the thinking of modern people and identified the tension between nature and freedom as an important ground motive. This tension, according to him, drives Westerners to experience alternately the extremes of breathtaking freedom or hopeless bondage to deterministic nature. Only the person who thinks from a creation/re-creation perspective can escape the power of this tension.

The American Christian apologist Dr F.A. Schaeffer (1912–84) also used this approach in his public discussions (though in personal talks he often moved on to involving the emotions). He spoke, not of 'ground motives', but of 'presuppositions' and held the view that in order to talk about the content of the gospel, you have to bring to the surface what you and your partners in discussion think, at the deepest level, about God, mankind, and history (cf. *The God Who is There*). Dick Keyes describes these presuppositions as 'foundational ideas, that are so close to us that they are like our eyeglasses: we do not see them, but we see the whole world through them' (in *True Heroism*, p.32).

The English writer C.S.Lewis (1898–1963) similarly challenged 'closed' thinking. He wrote that as soon as a person had come to accept that reality was not closed but open, and can be influenced by a totally 'other' reality, 'one may be in for anything' (*Miracles*, p.98).

b) In the sixties and seventies the climate became increasingly political. At this time of student revolutions and protests the central issue no longer concerned what one thought at the deepest level, but what one wanted at the deepest level. In this period the will and the motives became of central interest. What, for you, is the point of it all? What are you striving for? What are your ideals? And the Christian faith, too, was tested on its ideological content.

It was the time of unmasking underlying ideologies. The Dutch economist Bob Goudzwaard discussed the interrelationship between our hidden ideologies in *Idols of our Time*. The dialogue between Christians and unbelievers now included our 'sub-motives'. What are you trying to achieve, subconsciously? Also, see what you are achieving

— you are unconsciously contributing to the enrichment of the rich and the impoverishment of the poor; the destruction of the environment; the oppression of women!

In the confrontation between the Christian faith and the ideologies of communism, fascism and capitalism, it had to be clarified that, although Christianity had often compromised, the Christian faith is no ideology — it misses the essential charateristic of an ideology, namely to make truth and morality subordinate to a pragmatic ideal. On the contrary, Christ called us to submit our pragmatic ideals to him. When we pray, 'Your kingdom come', it does not mean that we are left behind with no work to do — we are called to erect 'signs of the kingdom'. But the kingdom itself comes 'from the other side'. It will be given to us, not created by us. So the power of the gospel breaks the power of ideologies.

c) **The eighties and nineties** brought another new perspective and we might scornfully call them the years of the 'I'-culture. But that is not completely fair. For they helped us to understand that a person is not only a thinking being and a striving being, but also a deeply feeling being. Often our feelings will determine our choices and convictions. They are by definition very personal. So in the eighties psychology came centre-stage.

Obsessive attention to the emotional side of personal being can degenerate into 'contemplating our navels' but it does not have to be so. It can bring to the surface a forgotten dimension which is of great importance, especially when seeking to understand why one person can believe while another person can't. It has been my experience, since the eighties, that by far the majority of serious conversations between believers and unbelievers involve

xviii this emotional level. When you ask, quite soberly, 'How do you *feel* about that?' in dialogue with those who do not believe, you can expect a fruitful exchange! The conversation I quoted at the beginning of this chapter took place in 1984 but since then has become a model for many similar exchanges. Today we have far fewer conversations about intellectual presuppositions or hidden motives. But most of my available time is now taken up discussing intuitive feelings and 'pre-monitions'.

Pre-monitions

From the outline above it is clear that although believers and non-believers have understood the importance of their different underlying presuppositions in dialogue, the importance of what I like to call underlying 'pre-monitions' has been largely neglected. When I use the word 'pre-monition', it is not as a synonym for 'premonition' (as we use it after a sudden, unexpected accident) — 'I had a premonition that something was going to go wrong'. No, I mean literally a 'pre-feeling', an often subconscious feeling which precedes my encounters and colours my openness to new discoveries. Such pre-feelings, intuitions, pre-monitions can be so strong that they can distort my ability to see reality for what it is.

It reminds me of the story about a psychiatric patient who believed that he was dead. All day long the man walked about and moaned, 'I am dead, I am dead'. In this way he escaped all responsibility and was eventually admitted to a psychiatric hospital. The psychiatrist treating him soon realized that the man's brain functioned quite properly.

So the psychiatrist set out to try and convince the man, by logic, that he was not dead but alive. He found a very convincing argument and said to the patient: 'Do you agree with me that when you prick the finger of a dead person, no blood will appear but only water?' The patient agreed. So the consultant quickly pricked the 'dead' man's thumb. A drop of blood squirted out. The patient stared at it with big eyes, turned to the doctor, and without a moment's hesitation exclaimed: 'Good gracious, I always believed dead people don't bleed but all this time I've been completely wrong!'

It is a good illustration of the fact that arguments do not necessarily convince — certainly not in dealing with strong pre-monitions. There is a deep unity between our thinking and feeling. To discern those background feelings we need to *listen* attentively, with perseverance and sympathy. If we ignore our subconscious feelings and fail to identify the pre-monitions that colour our thinking, we are in danger of leading a double life.

A Biblical View of Personhood

In the development of the debate between Christians and non-believers we have seen that different aspects of personal being have been centre-stage successively — intellect, will, and emotions. Does this mean that as human beings we are therefore fatally split? Does each person have three or more selves? (see also Ch. 8).

xx No, it is my assumption in this book that there is a unity between will, thinking, and feeling, for behind all the facets of personality is the heart. The book of wisdom in the Bible, Proverbs, calls the heart 'the wellspring of life' (4:23). The person whose heart is right achieves unity. True, such people are few and far between. When they speak out their thoughts these express exactly how they feel and when they express their feelings these are well thought through. People of such integrity have only one ideal and it is perfectly expressed by their will. Will, thinking, and emotion are in harmony. You may well ask whether it is possible to find even one such person. The Bible says there was only one, ever. The Apostle Paul calls him the only 'true adult' in his letter to the Ephesians (4:11–15) and urges us to grow up to 'the whole measure of the fullness of Christ'. This is how we achieve unity (v. 13) — with each other as Christians — but a unity surely based on having first found unity within ourselves.

Summary

Quite often if is clear that an exchange of ideas and facts does not help to transfer faith or make it acceptable. There are deep and often inexpressible, subconscious feelings involved. Sometimes people genuinely say, 'If only I could believe!' But it is possible to progress past this stalemate with persevering questions and sympathetic listening.

In the *fifties* most dialogues between believers and non-believers took place in the context of intellectual pre-suppositions — how you subconsciously *think* about things.

In the *sixties* the discussion shifted to subconscious motives and ideologies — what one strives to achieve — the *will*.

In the *eighties* the realization grew that *feelings* are very important and that these often form the final reasons why a person cannot believe or cannot grow in faith.

There has only ever been one completely mature person on the earth — we read about him in the New Testament letter to the Ephesians (4:13).

Questions

1. 'Faith is not just a sure knowledge . . . but also a firm trust'. Discuss this catechism answer in the light of the above chapter. Is it correct to differentiate between knowledge and trust? Include Bible readings from Hebrews 11 and Jeremiah 20.

2. Christ heals our dividedness'. Is there promise of complete healing? Or is that only for the future? What does it mean here and now? Compare this statement with the statement of F.A. Schaeffer in *True Spirituality*, that 'there is a promise of substantial healing'.

3. Discuss the shift from 'thinking' to 'feeling' as the basis for understanding personality. What are the pros and cons of each perspective?

xxii Bible Readings

Proverbs 4:23; Jeremiah 14:9–19; 20:7, 14–18; Matthew 6:10; Ephesians 4:11–15; Hebrews 11:1.

For Further Reading

Dooyeweerd, H. *Roots of Western Culture* (Toronto: Wedge Publishing Foundation, 1979)

Goudswaard, B. *Idols of our Time* (Downers Grove, Ill.: Intervarsity Press, 1984)

Keyes, D. *True Heroism* (Navpress, 1995)

—— *Beyond Identity* (Carlisle: Solway, 1997)

Lewis, C.S. *Undeceptions* (London: Geoffrey Bles, 1971)

—— *Miracles* (Fount Paperbacks, 1974)

Pascal, B. *Pensées* (Penguin Classics, 1966)

Schaeffer, F.A. 'The God Who is There', *The Complete Works of Francis A. Schaeffer, Vol. 1: A Christian View of Philosophy and Culture,* (Carlisle: Solway, 1995)

—— 'True Spirituality', *The Complete Works of Francis A. Schaeffer, Vol. 3: A Christian View of Spirituality,* (Carlisle: Solway, 1995)

1
Doubt and Certainty

Doubt rules. Today doubting is far more acceptable than claiming that we can know anything for certain. Society is suspicious of certainty, and if you dare to express it you might find yourself labelled a 'fundamentalist'.

Certainty is clearly dangerous; have we forgotten the evil perpetrated in the past in the name of who-knows-what beliefs? Certainty is frightening; we often hear someone say, 'Those overconfident people make my life a misery.' Certainty can be deceptive. Who knows how many millions of people have marched along in the triumphal processions of another 'certain' ideology — only to be disappointed and have their lives destroyed by chaos and the anarchy of war. To be sure, it's safer to doubt!

Historical Overview

During the early Enlightenment René Descartes (1596–1650) wrote his *Discourse on Method* to answer the question: how can I become certain? It explained his method of deliberate, systematic doubt to discern those facts which could be stated with absolute certainty from among the philosophies, world-views, and religions of his day. He started off by doubting everything and ruthlessly rejecting every assumed truth. By the end of the process his only remaining certainty was the fact of his doubt. For Descartes doubt was an intellectual matter, and so, according to his well-known definition of being, 'I think, therefore I am', he concluded that, thinking, he could only doubt. Therefore, doubting, I am! It is the only absolute certainty and on it all other certainties have to be built.

Today Descartes' 'method of doubting' is still the intellectually acceptable way for a modern person to find certainty — to examine all things critically and then to ask, 'Is it really like that?' The next step is to build only on that which was found to be certain. This attitude has infiltrated every area of life. But, whereas Descartes fervently believed that the great classical temple of knowledge would be rebuilt on his foundation of doubt, we in post-modern times have come to see those aims of Descartes and the Enlightenment as absolutely unattainable. No one sees a building of certainties arise on that foundation of doubt, and the ideals of modernism and of the Enlightenment are now considered folly — the mere word 'certainty' casts suspicion, whereas doubting is so common that few people realize how profoundly they doubt. Doubt has become our master.

Therefore it is important to analyse doubt: what is it? Is it true that the opposite of doubt is certainty? Are there different kinds of doubt? How does doubt affect the

Christian faith? We should ask all these questions also of certainty: what do we mean by certainty? Are there different kinds of certainty? And, most important of all, what is the relationship between doubt and certainty?

Doubt and Certainty

When we speak of doubt and certainty in the same breath we generally assume that certainty is the opposite of doubt. But is that true — is certainty the opposite of doubt?

I can remember how I learnt to enjoy boating. When I stepped into a rowing boat for the first time as a little boy of five, it immediately sank deeper into the water . . . I was terrified. Immediately you doubt whether the boat is really capable of holding you up, whether it is to be trusted at all. However, when you have rowed for a bit, or even better, have had someone you trust unconditionally to row you about for a while, inner peace returns. Your trust slowly increases. Keep going a bit longer and the adventure becomes fun, giving you a sense of great satisfaction — that it *is* possible to float on the water! You might even start rocking the boat, first gently, then quite wildly and with confident abandon.

During each new phase of the adventure you experience the same sequence of emotions. When I found myself on a yacht for the first time with the sails flapping, the boom narrowly missing my head, and the world tilting dangerously, I experienced similar terror and doubt — we were surely bound to capsize. But with practice and good instruction it all makes sense and soon you find it fun to sail as close to the wind as possible, fearlessly enjoying the spray in your face.

These examples clearly show that certainty is not the opposite of doubt, but rather, that courage and trust are. You need elements of certainty — knowing that the sails are in good condition, that there is a keel underneath the boat, that the ropes are strong enough. But the wind and dark water will always be unpredictable. Sailing is a skill you learn and it tests your courage and your nerve.

To me, believing is a bit like sailing. In sailing you dare to trust because by experience you have come to see that the boat can carry you safely over the waves and along with the wind. But at every new phase of the challenge moments come when you hold your breath and think, 'Will we stay afloat?' When you're sailing smoothly you feel happy and secure, but when the waves get too close upon each other or too high, or a wrong manoeuvre makes the boat tilt dangerously, you immediately feel doubt. The difference between this doubt and your initial doubt is the level of doubting (what you doubt) and how you experience the doubt ('I recognize this feeling'). Trust must be recovered again and again in order to progress. So also with the doubts of faith. In order to progress it is not certainty but trust which must be recovered again and again.

The rest of this chapter looks at how to identify your doubt and recover your trust, even in the midst of a storm.

What is Doubt?

Up to now I have defined doubt in terms of a lack of trust, following the analysis of Dr O. Guinness in his book, *Doubt*. This book appeared in the USA under the title *In Two Minds*, which is a good definition of doubt. The Latin word for 'two' is *duo* and, indeed, when you doubt you waver between two viewpoints. 'How long are you going to waver between two opinions?' the prophet Elijah asked the people of Israel on Mount Carmel (1 Ki. 18:21). That is doubt! You are drawn in two opposite directions at the same time; you experience contradictory emotions. In the case of Israel this was to worship both Jahweh *and* Baal; in the case of a person learning to sail it is to experience, simultaneously, feelings of 'yes, the boat will hold me up' *and* 'no, it will never stay afloat'.

The reason why Christians have a problem with handling doubt is that they often experience a deep sense that doubt is wrong, even sinful. Therefore many people suppress their fears and questions. Not daring to show their doubt they make it taboo. But this stunts their growth and progress. I prefer the approach of Helmut Thielicke who called doubt 'an envelope with a message inside it' — to find the message you need first to open the envelope.

In his book on doubt, Dr Guinness starts off by describing an experience in a Pyrenean village. A farmer had tied an enormous load of wood onto the back of a donkey. However hard the farmer whipped the animal, it could only stumble along, getting progressively slower and slower, until it sank down in exhaustion under the burden.

5

Still the farmer whipped the poor animal. The writer saw this as a parable of how some Christians treat their faith — they say, 'Believe this', 'Stop doubting', 'Act in faith' and continue to try and whip their faltering faith into action until, finally, it collapses and can go no further.

6   It is good to stop and ask whether you actually progress by whipping your faith and urging it on in this way. Sometimes it is better to ask the questions and allow the doubts out than to have your faith collapse under that burden. Part of life at L'Abri is our calling to encourage honest questions, even doubting ones, to the surface in our search for real answers. Doing this does not necessarily make life easier, but it is worthwhile to embark on the adventure of expressing that which is alive inside you. However, to deal honestly with your doubt it is important to discern and learn to verbalize *what* you doubt, what your deepest *questions* are, and what *situations* prompted your doubt.

Types of doubt

There are different *levels* of doubt. Superficial doubts relate to, for instance, indecision about what to wear or which video to watch. On a deeper level doubts concern how you spend your time or money. It becomes more complicated when you struggle with doubts about whom you can trust as a work partner, a friend, and ultimately, as a life-partner. The deepest level of doubt concerns the very meaning of existence — does life have meaning? Is there something sustaining it all? Is there anything trustworthy upholding us?

There are also many *causes* for doubt and Dr Guinness describes seven common causes which I will summarize here:

a) Not remembering. In the same way as the Old Testament people of Israel started doubting God when they could no longer remember clearly how he had saved them in the past, we too, when we forget how God helped us yesterday and the day before, sink into doubts about whether he can care for us today and tomorrow. Second or third generation Christians especially can easily forget the great things God has done for their ancestors and parents and doubt his existence — even while they are living on the basis of what God provided. Remembrance is the way back from doubt. 'Remembrance is the breathing of the soul,' says a Jewish proverb.

b) A wrong image of God. A child might pray to God, 'Heal my dad of cancer! And if you don't, I'll stop believing in you!' or, 'Give me a friend if you're really there' or, 'Let me get a letter this week if you're real.' What is our image of God when we make such requests? God as the great Father Christmas, at all times there to fulfil our every desire? Praying to God with a false image in mind can only lead to disappointment, which often precipitates a crisis of faith, and doubt. Then it is easy to throw out the baby with the bathwater — God together with the false image. Therefore, take time to learn who God really is so that you may be able to identify such false images. Test your image of God; keep listening to him, in order to get to know him better, and hear what he himself is saying to you.

c) Lack of knowledge. It might be that you have never seriously questioned why or what you actually believe. I once spoke to a catechism class of twelve- to fourteen-year olds and they were not inhibited in airing their opinions. One girl started: 'When I sit in church I sometimes wonder what I'm really doing there — is there really a God?' 'Wow', another girl answered, 'I also wonder whether God is there, but on the other hand, when I pray . . .' So I asked them the simple question how a person can be sure that God is there. 'No idea!' I asked why then they believed at all. 'Well, my father and mother taught me to believe . . .' But it gave them no assurance in their own belief — they doubted. They had deep feelings of alienation: 'Sometimes I think that God is not there at all.' They doubted because their belief in God had never had meaningful personal content. Belief, for them, was only a matter of 'how it feels to me'. But when their feelings changed, their faith changed too, so that 'When I feel it I have it, but when I don't feel it I've lost it.' When they stopped *feeling* their faith they doubted, because they never had meaningful reasons for believing. And there *are* good reasons to believe — I will discuss some at the end of this summary.

d) Lack of commitment. Dr Guinness illustrates this with what he had seen happen again and again when two people fell in love — they liked each other, spent more and more time together, felt sure that they were well-suited, and yet, as soon as marriage became a serious possibility, invariably they started to doubt their relationship. He noted with interest that their doubts disappeared as soon as the marriage certificate was signed and they knew that they were bound together 'in sickness and health; for better, for worse'. Why? Because the act of commitment assured them both of the solid intention of their partner to persevere responsibly in this relationship. But today many Christians treat their faith in the same way as a couple who are living together might treat their relationship — it is a good thing as long as it lasts, but they keep their options open to get out as soon as the relationship no longer lives up to their expectations. They are involved, but not committed. God gives his promise of assurance in the context of commitment: 'Whoever does my will shall know whether my teaching is from God', says Jesus (Jn. 7:17, cf. 1 Jn 2:3). Commitment stops doubt. In the same way as the wedding ring becomes an important symbol of the marriage commitment, in our life of faith, too, a physical symbol of dedication is important — a ritual, song, action, to testify to our commitment.

e) Lack of nourishment. How do you maintain a close friendship? How do you stay assured of your love for each other in a marriage relationship? By working at it. If you have not seen someone for two years it might take a while to feel comfortable in each other's company. A marriage relationship suffers unless you spend time with your partner. That is true for our relationship with God too. We need to work at maintaining it; it takes time. The Bible

9

uses many images to describe this aspect of perseverance in relating to God: running a race (where you have to keep fit and maintain your stamina) or fighting a battle (where you have to maintain your armour and continue to be alert).

f) Result of stress or strain. This reminds me of Elijah on Mount Carmel (1 Ki. 18). He astounded the whole nation of Israel by calling them publicly to account — 'How long will you waver between two opinions?' They chose *for* God, and Jezebel responded with persecution. But Elijah's next reaction was to sink into a deep depression — he lay down in the desert, without hope, and said, 'I am finished. I cannot handle life any more. God, take me away.' However, God sent him on, to Horeb, and there appeared to him in the gentle whisper of a breeze — God's special therapy for Elijah's doubt! This doubt is typical of the doubt that might attack believers after a period of intense strain or stress. Then they need the therapy of 'Go, rest, sleep.' Jesus recommended it to his tired and stressed disciples. Sometimes doubt is best treated by very practical and mundane remedies — go out for a moment, stop working, eat a square meal, have an early night.

g) Result of trauma. You might have grown up in an environment which severely impaired your trust; with experiences which, although now in the past, still make it hard for you to trust. These experiences will affect your ability to believe, for trust is the opposite of doubt. Two kinds of trauma most often damage trust. First there are

the many possible causes of an *emotional blockage* to trust —
psychological manipulation, misuse of trust, shame, abuse,
inferiority feelings, fear. Second, trust is often damaged as
a result of *bereavement*. It is a normal part of grief to feel
that 'God does not exist — he has never been — and he
never will be! I can't feel him, and I don't know him.' The
person who feels like this has grown cold, emotionally. We
read about them in the Bible — for instance, Jacob whose
heart stayed cold when he heard that Joseph, his son, was
alive in Egypt (Gn. 45:25–28). To regain trust after such a
painful bereavement takes time and often involves going
back to where your trust first derailed.

Reasons for believing

I think it is very important for us to open up the envelope
of doubt and take out the message, knowing the good
news of God's generous offer: that we may fire all our
questions at him without fear of rejection. Just look at
how Jesus treated people. No one was rejected by him
with, 'You can't ask that!' Jesus never said, 'Believe, or I
shoot!' He always entered into the real question with real
arguments. I know that rationalism can be dangerous —
arranging everything in neat logical order — but I am
concerned that we should not give up seriously examining
the evidence there is for answering as basic a question as
whether God exists.

So, how can we know that God exists? Sometimes we
cannot accept a 'higher' fact because we lack the information which logically precedes it, the 'lower' truth. In the
time of Copernicus, for instance, people could not believe

that the earth turns around its own axis at a great speed because they lacked knowledge about magnetism and gravity. In the same way many people cannot believe in a personal God who affects real-life history because they think of the world as a closed system of cause and effect. From a young age they might have absorbed the idea that all things are caused to happen from within the system. When something happens which cannot be explained by cause and effect they label it as 'impossible'. This strong prejudice obstructs their ability to believe the 'higher' truth; it is a barrier that keeps people from finding God and that needs to be broken down to allow them to come to faith — by a demolition of 'arguments and every pretension that sets itself up against the knowledge of God' (2 Cor. 10:5).

For there *are* good reasons to believe! Dr Schaeffer summarized them by pointing to two phenomena– the form of the universe, and the 'mannishness of man'.

a) The form of the universe. There is unity and diversity in the physical reality in which we live. The laws of nature make rational sense — some One must have designed them; they are reasonable. Or can you believe that the design and colours of the peacock's feathers, or the complexity of a human eye, are the products of time and chance? Even Darwin had problems to believe that when he considered the human eye!

b) The 'mannishness of man'. There is a universal deep longing in the hearts of people for enduring meaning in their existence, for personal identity that will not vanish like a drop of water that falls into the ocean. If there were nothing to satisfy that longing we would indeed be living in a warped universe which seems sadistically to equip its creatures only for self-torment. But Ecclesiastes says that God has 'planted eternity in the hearts of men' (3:11). Mankind in its 'mannishness' — its longings, conscience, inner conflicts, awareness of identity, sense of eternity — is a living witness to the truth of God's existence and providence; the good news of God fits the needs of our human existence as a glove fits a hand.

13

Simplified three-part description of doubt

In order to remember the different types of doubt I have simplified Dr Guinness's list and divided it into three groups, distinguishing between doubts of the *will*, doubts of the *mind*, and doubts of the *emotions*. Such a division has the added advantage that it corresponds to my understanding of what it means to be human — to have a will, mind, and emotions

a) **Will** An unsigned contract serves well to illustrate the role that the will plays in doubt. The Bible is striking in the severity with which it treats doubts of the will — it is without pardon. When trying to understand their doubt many people immediately turn to James 1: 'He who doubts is like a wave of the sea . . . that man should not think he will receive anything from the Lord.' It is followed by the words 'unstable in all he does' — which, clearly, speak about doubts of the will. James is here speaking about the person who does not want to act in accordance with what has become transparently clear to them — a person who understands, but refuses to act in accordance with that understanding. If you want to be sure of God you have to seek after him, says Jeremiah, with your whole heart and if you do not do it with your whole heart, then you will not find him (Je. 29:13). You must be prepared to say, 'God, if you are really there, I am on your side whatever it may mean for me.' If you dare not say that, 'do not call yourself a doubter, rather a stubborn one', says Pascal (*Pensées*). Doubts of the will are often used as camouflage by stubborn people, stubbornly defending stubborn ideas.

b) Mind. The Bible treats doubts of the mind quite severely, but with exceptions. On the one hand God calls people to question him — 'Ask of me!' (Je. 29:12, Matt. 7:7). On the other hand God treats continual doubts of the mind as deep-seated sin and the sign of a broken relationship with him. On the one hand God generously opens himself up for questioning — 'test all things and hold on to that which is good' (1 Thes. 5:21) — to test means to analyse, to ask pointed questions. On the other hand, we are not free to set our own autonomous intellect above God's and to say, 'Lord God, now *you* have to justify yourself to me.' When Job fell into such an attitude, God reversed roles and said, 'Job, do you think that you are the judge over me?' (38:3). Today such a critical attitude is very real — we dare God to appear before the throne of our reason where he has to justify himself to us, or we care little for believing in him. But is it reasonable for us to set our intellect above that of the Creator of all thought and mind and being?

c) **Emotions.** The Bible is most gentle in dealing with emotional doubt — there is hardly any condemnation. When they read in James 1, 'He who doubts is like a wave of the sea . . . that man should not think he will receive anything from the Lord', people with emotional doubt immediately feel hopeless — they interpret it as meaning that they are expected to pray to God only when they are completely without doubt. How can they ever pray? Indeed, they doubt and feel therefore in a deadlock. But James addressed doubts of the will. I believe that the final verses of the book of Jude which say, 'Be merciful to those who doubt', deal with emotional doubt — they are in a very different tone from the words in James 1! Again and again I find this attitude in the Bible when people are emotionally unable to believe. When Jesus appears to all his disciples they 'could not believe it for joy'. However, Jesus did not reprimand them. Instead he encourages them, understands them, and says 'Give me bread and fish, then I will eat here in front of your eyes.' To Thomas he says, 'Come here and put your hand in my wound.' He invites them to become certain through observation, by using their senses. God does the same in Psalm 73; and Job's response (Jb. 42:5) is based on a similar experience.

Certainty

As a result of the far-reaching influence of natural science, it has become common today to speak of certainty only in

15

the context of scientific proof. Such proofs are based on observation by the senses, measurements by instruments, technology, and logically deduced conclusions. We all share the presupposition that $2 \times 2 = 4$ is empirical and certain, and that such certainty is the opposite of doubt.

16   But I believe it is wrong to limit certainty like that. For two reasons. First, there are innumerable *certainties*, every day, all around us, which *cannot be explained scientifically* in calculations and formulae. For example, I love my wife — this is something that cannot be proved by a process of measurement. Or consider beauty — I can be certain that one painting is beautiful while another one is obviously ugly. But I cannot express it in a watertight formula. The same is true of the certainty that something is fair or unjust — it is closer to the wisdom of Solomon than to purely scientific calculations (or justice quickly degenerates into legalism). A mother is one hundred per cent sure that she loves her child, but cannot prove it empirically. We all experience certainty in relation to beauty, love, trust, and that makes me critical of the idea that all certainty *must* be capable of expression in the $2 \times 2 = 4$ fashion.

Second, and of more technical interest, *scientists* themselves today *question certainty* - even science is now seen as relative and based on underlying, particular assumptions which define a specific environment for interpretation. In this way scientific certainty is based on trust plus facts, and not on facts alone. Is it not astounding that while ordinary people have such a rigid image of what scientific certainty is ($2 \times 2 = 4$), the scientists say that things are not nearly so certain, but that they depend on the paradigms within which a particular theorem functions. As an example, what is light? One interpretation describes it in terms of particles, another in terms of waves. It has been proved that time exists as a relative measure and chaos has been shown to have an inner order of its own. With uncertainty abounding in those things which *can* be measured and formulated, certainty remains the secret of the Maker.

17

Certainty in faith

When we think about certainty we must be careful not to be influenced by the (false) image of empirical certainty. Certainty in matters of faith is linked with trust; and trust is something which can be shocked, which needs to be maintained, and which may be questioned. Such certainty can grow but it can also be damaged in a single moment — it is a living thing. Assurance in our faith needs to be fed or it becomes frail and sickly.

You might well ask how we can know for certain that we are dealing with God and not just with our own imaginings. There are two answers to this. The *traditional* answer is that we can know, objectively, by testing what we think we know about God against what the Bible says about him. The Bible is our standard. The truth of what we feel or imagine or think or wish about God should always be measured by this standard: is it in accordance with the way God revealed himself in the Bible? But not everybody shares the conviction that the Bible is the word of God. If you were to ask me, 'How did *you* become certain?' I would give a *general* answer based on the good reasons for believing that I have already discussed. But I would add a second answer, a more *personal* one. It helped me very much to discover that, in using the Bible to answer the question of how to be certain of the existence of God, the Apostle Paul again and again turned the question around. In his letter to the Corinthians (1 Cor. 8:1–3) he says: 'What? . . . we know him? Rather, we *are* known by him!' People often recognized Jesus as the Son of God when they experienced that Jesus knew them intimately — their unspoken fears and hopes, their fall-enness and potential for restoration — and that he loved them in that complete knowledge. They experienced his unconditional acceptance (e.g. Zaccheus, Lk. 19). What makes me certain in my faith that I am dealing with God, are those moments when I meet myself in Scripture and experience, deep in my heart, 'Yes, this is *me* — I am known by God!' (Ps. 139, Gal. 4:9).

Becoming certain

In *scientific* knowledge, scientists achieve certainty in their study of a subject by making measurements, noting down their observations, thinking about and comparing their notes, and finally expressing these as conclusions or postu-lates. They use their logic to deal with the sub-human reality they are studying. But when it comes to *personal* knowledge, we can never know another person by ob-jective measurements, observations, or logical conclusions — for the essential components of the heart and mind cannot be measured. We can get to know another person only to the extent that they reveal the contents of their heart and mind to us. It can never be a completely one-sided affair, for that person will share personal information only if we respond in an appropriate way, ask the right questions, create a sense of empathy. Only as I give myself to another can they know me, and only as they give themselves to me can I know them. Growing in our knowledge of each other takes mutual, continual self-giving.

It is exactly the same with God. God makes himself known to us, but it is only as we respond and open up ourselves to him that we can know him with more certainty. Consider how far God transcends us. If you want to get to know the Queen of England personally you are dependent on her goodwill. No one can decide they want to get to know the Queen — it is something *she* decides. But even if she is willing to make herself known, the initiative is one-sided and can lead to a meeting only when you respond to her invitation. How much more so with God! By grace he makes himself known to us. We can never know him by our own will-power, feelings, or understanding. *He* comes to us. But we will know him with certainty only as *we* open ourselves up in response to what the Son teaches us about the Father through the Spirit.

Summary

Today it is more acceptable to doubt than to be certain. Methodical doubt was developed by René Descartes during the Enlightenment as a technique for achieving certainty. Now not even scientific 'absolutes' are certain any longer.

20

However, trust, not certainty, is the opposite of doubt. Different causes for doubt can be identified in the areas of will, understanding and emotions. The Bible treats wilful doubt very seriously; intellectual doubt less severely. Jesus was always very gentle in dealing with those who suffered emotional doubt. To find certainty of faith involves not just a biblical knowledge of God, but also a personal experience of being known by God. It is as we respond to God, by continually opening ourselves to learn more from him, that we grow in our assurance and trust.

Questions

1. What everyday things do you treat as certain and how did you become certain of them?
2. How do you get to know another person? Can you use similar methods to get to know God?
3. To which of the seven causes of doubt in *In Two Minds* do these examples of doubt belong — Gen 15:8; Jdg. 6:17; Mtt. 11:3; Jn 11:30; Acts 12:14,15?
4. The only thing Descartes was certain of was his doubt. What Christian truths are certain beyond doubt? (cf. Gen 3:19; Ps 8:6; Ec. 3:3; Rom. 8:20; 1Tim. 6:7, etc.)

Bible Readings

Genesis 45:25–28; 1 Kings 18; Job 40; 42:5; Psalms 73; 139; Jeremiah 29:12,13; Matthew 7:7; John 7:17; Luke 19; Galatians 4:9; 1 Corinthians 8:1–3; 1 Thessalonians 5:21; James 1; 1 John 2:3; Jude 22.

For Further Reading

Bavinck, H. *The Certainty of Faith* (Ontario: Paideia Press, 1980)

Descartes, R. 'Discourse on Method', *The Philosophical Works*, ed. E.S. Haldane and G.R.T.Ross, 1 (Cambridge, 1911)

Guinness, O. *In Two Minds* (Downers Grove, Ill.:InterVarsity Press, 1976)

Habermas, G.R. *Dealing with Doubt* (Chicago: Moody Press, 1990)

McGrath, A. *Doubt, Handling it honestly* (Downers Grove, Ill.: Inter-Varsity Press)

Newbiggin, L. *Proper Confidence* (Grand Rapids, MI: Eerdmans, 1995)

Pascal, B. *Pensées* (Penguin Classics, 1966)

Vande Beukel, A. *More Things in Heaven and Earth* (London: SCM Press Ltd., 1991)

2

Dealing with Disappointment

When my conversation with a person who seriously tried to understand the Christian faith ended in her exclamation, 'If only I could believe!', she did not mean that Christianity was too complicated to understand or that the Bible stories were too far removed from her twentieth-century lifestyle to have relevance for her. She had a genuine, serious interest in the Christian faith, and her words remind me of what is written in the Bible about the patriarch Jacob. When he heard the good news that his son Joseph was still alive, 'Jacob was stunned; he did not believe them' (Gn. 45:25–28). Today, and maybe especially today, when people hear the good news of the gospel, sadly, they often can't believe it. But why not?

When the Bible says that Jacob 'did not believe them', this might imply that he did not *dare* to believe their words, *dare* to trust them. To believe is to trust. The Hebrew verb for believing, *aman*, comes from the same root as our English word 'amen'. To 'say amen' to something means to consider it trustworthy. Jacob could not do that at first because his trust had been damaged. Perhaps more than once in the past he had heard rumours that

Joseph was still alive, but on closer investigation he was disappointed, every time. Now, however much he wanted to, he dared not trust another rumour! More than that — he could not. There is a close link between disappointment in the past and an inability to trust in the present.

The Nature of Being Human

If trust is so crucial to our being, and if disappointment has such power to damage trust, why then in the past has so little attention been paid to the significant effects of disappointment on our lives?

I believe that our understanding of disappointment and trust is shaped by our subconscious view of what it means to be human. If we see people as robots, we interact with them in a mechanical way — education and child-rearing become matters of technique. Alternatively, if we see people as rationally endowed animals, we concentrate on producing rational arguments — to persuade and manipulate them. If we see people as herd-animals we seek to control them — who is in charge becomes the only important issue. Each approach is based on an underlying view of what it is to be human.

What then does the Bible teach us about being human? It begins in Gn. 1:27 with: 'So God created man in his own image . . . male and female he created them.' God made the animals 'according to *their* kinds' but he made the first people 'in *his own* image'! Being human is a unique kind of being. But what does this mean? The 'image' of God used to be explained in terms of qualities human beings seemed to have uniquely, and which they did not share with other kinds of creatures — 'man is a rational-moral being' was the generally accepted definition.

24 In fact, this definition comes from the Greek philosopher Aristotle (384–322 BC). He laid the foundation for Western thinking. His definition of 'being human' left no space for the emotions — and so he was largely responsible for the fact that disappointment came to be considered an unimportant part of human experience. Aristotle also influenced traditional church teaching so that the person who cannot believe, as we have seen, came to be considered lacking in either understanding (reason) or will (morals). But to classify all inability to believe as either ignorance or proud and sinful unwillingness to believe is a biased reaction, based on an incomplete understanding of what it truly means to be human.

Contrary to Aristotle's view, the 'image' of God in human beings includes the emotions. Without emotions we cannot be true representatives of God on earth — which is at the heart of a biblical understanding of what it is to be human. We are called to reach beyond our human selves in order to represent God on the earth — as his image-bearers, to bring *him* glory. In the Garden of Eden God motivated the first man and woman by setting them a task and giving them a vision. Adam and Eve were called, together, to develop and conserve the earth that it might grow from a paradise-garden into a garden-city.

For me, therefore, the French-Jewish philosopher Emmanuel Levinas (1906-95) is closer to biblical truth when he describes the essence of what it is to be human with the word *le désir* — longing. We are all filled with deep longings. We are not robots or animals. But each person, as a unique human being, has the longing to give themselves, freely and by their own choice, in various relationships of trust. We also have deep longings to give shape and form to our environment during the journey of life on which God has placed us, from paradise to kingdom, the way that leads to the City of Peace (Rev. 21).

If this journey had continued undisturbed, our relationship of trust with God, ourselves, other people, the creatures around us, and the earth would have deepened and strengthened. But the Bible vividly describes how, soon after creation, the serpent attacked this basic trust and undermined it. How was it done? Quite cleverly, by casting doubt on the trustworthiness of God and arousing a perverse desire for the wrong object. Disappointment followed. Trust was derailed; and all the supporting relationships of trust collapsed.

Vulnerability

The biblical account of our pre-history shows that our vulnerability as human beings is the result, not only of intellectual and moral inadequacy, but also of a fiendishly successful attack on our basic trust. In the subsequently fallen world (the serpent succeeded, after all) trust has become our most vulnerable characteristic — it is threatened from without and damaged from within. There is no simple solution; we need more than a pointed reminder: 'Learn to trust.' To trust is more difficult than we often realize!

But blind trust is not a blessing either, certainly not in a fallen world. You cannot live without caution. You need to be careful, even mistrustful, at times. We don't respect someone who embraces every stranger, accepts every offer, believes every promise. And we don't think very highly of a person who buys the first car they come across or who joins the first prospective partner they meet! Such a person needs to be warned and protected; shielded from certain ruin. The Bible is quite realistic about the need for caution in the spiritual realm too: 'Dear friends, do not believe every spirit, but test the spirits to see whether they are from God' (1 Jn. 4:1).

Disappointment

Disappointment hurts our basic trust. If a deep need is not met or our expectations never materialize, we subconsciously create a protective layer around our longings. We dare not be disappointed another time — we dare not trust again. How can we grow in trust despite our painful and humiliating disappointments? How can we incororate our disappointments into a living trust?

Our ability to handle our disappointments is intimately related to our ability to trust. We have seen how Jacob, when he heard the good news about Joseph his son, was too stunned to believe it — and this may well have been as a result of his past disappointments.

Because disappointment is such a painful personal experience we try to evade it — by ignoring it. But disappointment affects our ability to trust, and trust is essential to every relationship. How we handle our disappointments therefore has an enormous effect on our *interpersonal relationships*. Even more important, it can affect our *relationship with God* — our ability to trust him — hence, 'if only I could believe!'

Longings

The Christian psychologist Larry Crabb discusses the problem of disappointment in his book *Inside Out*. He begins by describing a typical church congregation as a community where relationships are superficial — no great disagreements, but no intimacy either; geniality and small talk, yes, but many people secretly suffer because of impersonal relationships. They do not know what others feel; neither can they make their own feelings known. Such superficial relationships gnaw away at the heart of the church community and make communication increasingly shallow, empty, and unsatisfactory. The same pattern can repeat itself in the community of the family or the community of the workplace. Why? In answer to that Crabb suggests that we need to explore 'the longings of our soul'. We need to ask what we had expected of each other when we joined, what were our unspoken longings and desires, what did we hope to achieve, and how did we expect others to fit in with our hopes and needs?

Crabb uses an illustration with three concentric circles to represent what he calls our 'casual', 'critical', and 'crucial' longings respectively:

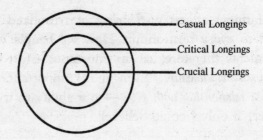

The 'casual longings' consist of our normal physical needs — for food, drink, sleep, and good health. These needs can be met independently; no interpersonal relationships are involved. The 'critical longings' represent those deeper needs which can only be met in relationship with other people — for meaningful work, dignity, appreciation, and intimacy. Finally, the third circle represents our 'crucial longings', the 'most profound longings of the human heart, those desires that must be met if life is to be worth living', the deep yearning of every human being for everlasting peace and constant security. 'Our hearts are restless in us until we find rest in God' (Augustine, *Confessions*). The writer of Ecclesiastes says something similar: 'He (God) has also set eternity in the hearts of men' (3:11). And Psalm 42 compares the deep desire every person has for a love-relationship with the eternal God to the thirsting of a wild deer for clear and cool running water.

Interpersonal disappointment

If the primary needs of the first 'casual' circle are not met a person experiences degrees of uncomfortable irritation.

Without sufficient rest you immediately notice that you feel uneasy and become short-tempered — you've been kept awake and need to do something about it. Usually you will find a solution. But if the deeper longings of the second 'critical' circle are not met, people are affected far more profoundly. These needs make us so vulnerable that it is only with great difficulty we can even acknowledge our hurt. Failure to satisfy these longings cause us painful interpersonal disappointment.

Escape routes and wrong strategies. We often try to escape from the place of our disappointment. We may try to find a substitute to compensate us for the unfulfilled desire or the disappointed expectation; sometimes material things can give us a 'quick fix'. Alternatively we may flee into anger and cynicism to cover up our disappointment and hurt. Or we may simply crowd disappointment out of our lives by being obsessively busy. However, such attempts to escape always result in interpersonal relationships that are shallow and flat, leaving us feeling alienated, like outsiders. If disappointment is ignored it takes its own revenge. Like a bushfire that smoulders unnoticed it erupts with great destructive force, now here, then there. Here are two imaginary but typical examples:

- When *Priscilla Smith* arrived in town she immediately started looking for a suitable church. She finally joined a congregation which had been positively recommended by several people and she had high expectations of her involvement there — especially since she never fitted very well in her previous church.

29

Six months later almost all her expectations had been disappointed. She had not made a single new friend — everyone seemed to walk past her witout noticing. When she was asked to lead her home-group Bible study one evening she chose Revelation 3: 'because you are luke-warm — neither hot nor cold — I am about to spit you out of my mouth'. The other members of the group could not understand what she was trying to say and left it at that though one older person was heard to mumble, 'Who does she think she is?'

This example is a clear illustration of what happens when we handle our disappointments badly. Priscilla's aggressive strategy caused only more superficial relationships. When she covered up her angry disappointment she also covered her openness to others. She experienced no intimacy or sense of belonging, and other members of the group sensed that 'something's bugging her'. True, for underneath the surface disappointment was hurting and irritating her. As long as she ignored it, it continued to develop into a grudge, a root of bitterness. And where such feelings are hidden from the outside, as Jesus said to the Pharisees, 'the cup is dirty on the inside', and, 'first clean the inside of the cup' (Mtt. 23:26).

• *Dave Matthews* is a truck driver. His younger brother is a lawyer. Dave always thinks to himself, 'I *should* have achieved more, I *could* have achieved more!' When his son turns out to be a bright student, all Dave's expectations are transferred to his boy. Will *he* achieve where Dave had failed? But the boy chooses a creative career instead of a legal profession and, as a result, his father is forever finding fault with him when he comes home. The boy feels a complete failure in the eyes of his father and, in order to survive, breaks all ties with home and goes his own way — the son has lost his father and the father is left to grow bitter, mourning the loss of his son. Why did it happen?

Because Dave never dealt with his own disappointment. His expectations, first of himself and then of his son, failed to materialize. Instead of recognizing and accepting this failure, he adopted a wrong strategy — one of irritation, manipulation, self-isolation and bitterness.

Victim and Sinner. We are so vulnerable in the area of our secret longings that we dare not acknowledge our bitter disappointments. We feel guilty about them. It is therefore like a breath of fresh air to find a way out which does not start off with condemning our sinfulness; on the contrary, Larry Crabb starts off by showing how we have all become victims. We have all experienced situations which disappointed our deepest longings and failed to meet our deepest needs — it's happened to me, you, and every person who has ever lived.

Christians especially should not be surprised at this. After all, Christians know how we have come to live in such a fallen and broken world and as victims of the fallenness, for instance, you never *could* get the training you so badly wanted (as happened to many people during World War II) — it is sad, and it is real. That is why there are families in which the children suffer, and church congregations in which people feel lonely and misunderstood. Yes, we all have become victims. And it hurts to be a victim, to be wounded in my deepest longings and expectations.

But how *can* we cope with such deep disappointment? Like Priscilla, we could voice our unhappiness and disgruntlement; when this happens under a 'spiritual' guise (such as a Bible study) it can be a powerful way of 'hitting back'. Like Dave, we could try to manipulate others; but that may well rebound in suppressed anger, bitterness, and more pain. People who suffer from disappointment can always be diagnosed by a loss of intimacy — seen in their superficial relationships, their masks and distrust.

Each person bears responsibility for the way in which they act in their own life situation. In my experience of bitter disappointments I am a *victim*, but in the way I react to my disappointment I often become a *sinner* — in the escape routes and shortcuts, the wrong turnings and disguises, disgruntlement and bitterness I prefer to adopt. When I use such sinful strategies in my disappointment, they invariably produce greater pain. But in that I alone am guilty; I can blame no one else for my actions. I alone am reponsible for my behaviour, my wrong choices, my sinful reactions. Paul writes to the Galatians (6:4,5): 'Each one should test his own actions . . . for each one should carry his own load' (cf. Gal. 6:2!).

Is there a way out? Is disappointment a fatal obstacle? Is there no hope for intimacy? Or is there a way out?

Fortunately there is a way which brings healing — not immediately and not completely. It will be slow but substantial. And there are steps along that way, as Larry Crabb put it:

- When you notice that your relationships are becoming superficial, '*admit confusion*'. It is much better to say 'Hold on, I cannot handle what is happening to me. *Help!*', than to continue covering up your feelings of confusion by wrong and self-destructive strategies. At this point you open the way to honest self-examination when you pray: 'Search me, O God, and know my heart; test me and know my anxious thoughts. See if there is any fault in me, and lead me in the way everlasting' (Ps. 139:23,24). In praying this you ask, not just for the willingness to be tested and corrected, but for God himself to come to you. He alone can show you what is inside your heart and open up ways of blessing for you. The realization of your incompleteness, your wrong thoughts and your perverse actions, then transforms your disappointment into hope for a better way. And when you hope you have already started to reverse the crippling effects of badly handled disappointment.

- '*Acknowledge disappointment*'. Allow the pain to surface. Make an effort to penetrate and *verbalize* to yourself and eventually to others what disappointed you. Say it aloud. What did you hope for? What did you expect of that congregation? What did you expect of yourself? What were the ideals and dreams you had for your partner . . . your children . . . your career? What is it that you yearned for? Larry Crabb calls it 'becoming aware of your thirst' and encourages his readers to 'stop pretending and face your deep longings'.

• Start building real relationships and stop protecting yourself. Admit that you have been inadequate and have failed. '*Accept correction*'. Then build openness into your relationships.

34

It is clearly difficult to follow this route and deal with your disappointments. It is the way of 'dying to yourself'. But it is also the way of being set free from the tyranny of disappointment, for when you verbalize your disappointment you bring it into the light and it loses its power over you. The person who has the courage to follow this way will find that it becomes the way into the hearts of others, the way into deeper trust and greater intimacy. It is the way which leads to new blessings because it is the way by which we experience, here and now, something of the 'way everlasting', the way of the everlasting LORD of Psalm 139!

Disappointment with God

We have now come to the third circle in the diagram of Larry Crabb, the area of 'crucial longings'. In this area we are disappointed, not in the circumstances or people around us, but in God. It is a deep and painful disappointment which often underlies the sincere cry, 'If only I could believe!'

Escape routes and wrong strategies. Not surprisingly, the same kind of strategies operate when we are disappointed in God as when we are disappointed in ourselves or other people. But it happens at a deeper level because our crucial longings are hidden so much deeper than our critical longings.

Here, too, the external symptom of our disappointment is a superficial relationship. People often say (maybe you've said it yourself), 'O yes, there is probably a God . . .' Just a passing thought; not worth thinking about any further. A person may be so desperately disappointed in God that they refuse even to mention him. I think it is accurate to say that in the same way public conversations about sexuality and sex were made taboo in Victorian times, God-talk in public is taboo today. If it is easy to slip into superficial relationships with other people because of our past disappointments, how much more so with God? How often we hide from God, even though he is closer to us than we are to ourselves — he is the One with whom we should be most intimate, the One we should love more than anyone or anything else. Why become so indifferent to him? Here are two examples, one biblical, one from the twentieth century:

• The two people on the road from Jerusalem to Emmaus after the Good Friday of the crucifixion and death of Jesus, were deeply disappointed. Their expectations of Jesus had been dashed. As they walked along that day they did not realize that the Risen One had joined them because 'they were kept from recognizing him' (Lk. 24:16). He was right there with them but they had no eyes to see him. How could it happen? In Lk. 24:21 we read what kept them from recognizing him — 'but we had hoped that he was the one who was going to redeem Israel'. Their expectations had been disappointed — what they had hoped for turned out to be nothing.

Yes, they had known a deep yearning for the liberation of the nation of Israel, for victory over death and the coming of the messianic kingdom of peace. For all of this they had put their hope in Jesus. But what had happened? Their Messiah ended up on the cross! Nothing happened remotely resembling the change they were waiting for — no kingdom of peace, no victory over death. Gone was all their hope. Not even the news of the resurrection could move them. Yes, they had heard the reports of the eye-witnesses of an empty tomb, but no one had come across *him* (v. 24). Even as Jesus was walking next to them they could not believe that he was alive. Their disappointment so engulfed them that they could not trust any good news. They had closed their hearts to what God could possibly be doing.

And they had closed their eyes to the Glorious One walking right next to them. Jesus calls them 'slow of heart'. Out of self-protection? Or despair? They resemble John the Baptist who had started full of faith but later doubted whether Jesus really was the Messiah (Mt. 11:2,3). He too had had high hopes of Jesus. But when these did not materialize in the way he had expected he was deeply disappointed. Even John, then, could no longer recognize the hand of God, (Mt. 11:4-6).

• The French philosopher Jean-Paul Sartre (1905-80) wrote a play called 'The Devil and God' in which he put the following words in the mouth of his main character, the rebel leader General Goetz:

> I pleaded, I begged for a sign. I sent messages to heaven, but no answer came. Heaven does not even know my name. All the time I asked myself what I could be in the eyes of God. Then, in a moment, I knew it: I am nothing. God does not see me. God does not hear me. God does not know me. Do you see the empty space above our heads? That is God. Do you see the space of the open doorway? That is God. Do you see that hole in the ground? That, too, is God. The silence is God. The absence is God. God is the loneliness of all the people. There is no one besides me; I have decided for evil, I have discovered good. I alone!

These words of doubt are followed by the well-known Sartrean saying — 'If God exists, man is nothing — if man exists . . . .' We are left to conclude for ourselves that, 'then God is nothing' — a hole, emptiness, absence!

But when I read the words of Goetz I interpret them as being autobiographical. Was there not, behind the scathing atheist Sartre, someone who had searched for God, again and again, someone who had hoped to find God and who was deeply disappointed when God did not answer him as he was expected to . . . ?

Victim and sinner. How should we deal with such unbelief? Traditionally all unbelief is treated as either ignorance or proud and sinful unwillingness to submit to God. But I do not think we should immediately judge the words of an unbeliever in that light. No atheist was born an atheist. Many experiences (also in relation to believers) could have contributed to their disappointed expectations of God. We should therefore look deeper into their disappointment and try to understand unbelief from the inside.

38 It is also what Jesus did. Have you ever noticed how little Jesus reprimanded his disciples for not believing the early reports of his resurrection? When he suddenly stands in their midst, they are terrified. 'Why are you troubled and why do doubts rise in your minds?' Jesus asks them (Lk. 24:38), not as an accusation but as a challenge and invitation. He wanted only to remove their fears, to help them worship him, the real Jesus, not their idol. So he makes himself available to them and says, 'Look at my hands and feet. It is I myself. Touch me and see.' And when the disciples for sheer joy and amazement could still not believe it (v. 41), he just accepts them. He even ate some fish in front of their eyes to prove that he was no ghost! In the same way we too can start by accepting our unbelief and the distrust with which we try to protect ourselves from disappointment — it may only disguise our deep longing for God.

We were all born into a fallen world, we all grew up in a thoroughly rationalistic culture, and now we all live at the stark and secularized end of the twentieth century. It has spoilt our longing for God and as such, though we are *sinners*, we all are *victims* too.

Is there a way out? So, is it all bad news? Are we left to be disappointed with God? No, for there is a way back to God. You alone are responsible for the way you handle your disappointments, also your disappointment with

God, and for the wrong strategies you use to try and cover your deep longing and need for him. There is a way back to him and Larry Crabb describes the steps along that way:

- '*Acknowledge the pain* in your heart.' Go back to your disappointment. Ask yourself what you longed for when you started to read the Bible. What did you hope to receive from God when you asked him to guide your life? For what did you cry out to him? What answer did you expect? And what answer did you get? Go back, too, to the longing which is still living deep inside you. Psalm 42 says, 'As the deer pants for streams of water, so my soul pants for you, O God.' Go back and name your deepest longings.

- '*Work at the problem* in your life.' Behind your disappointment in God there often hides a problem in your life or in the world around you — a problem which caused you to have an unrealistic or wrong expectation of God. You might have had distorted ideals, images, or desires in your faith. If you examine your expectations of God they are often unhealthy, immature, or selfish. You may have expected God to give you that which you felt your parents, associates, or friends owed you. You may have expected God to fill the vacuum left by others — sometimes he does it; sometimes, not. Sometimes God encourages you to tackle the problem *yourself* and learn to trust him in a new way as you take up your own responsibilities.

- '*Stop sinning*.' When you have named your disappointment and identified the problem in your life, you often come to see how wrong you were in your expectations of God. You may have thought that it was God's responsibility, in his omnipotence, to satisfy all your desires — just as young children expect their mother to satisfy all their needs, all the time. But when you have identified your self-centredness you will have to change your behaviour!

40

It is precisely to set us free from an endless spiral of self-centredness that Jesus commands us to 'seek first his (God's) kingdom and his righteousness, and all these things will be given to you as well' (Mt. 6:33). 'All these things' — all these expectations to which we cling in our small faith — are fulfilled, freely, as bonus, when we search for God him*self*. What is really important to God is that in our relationship with him we die to ourselves, not by self-hatred or abusing our bodies, but by letting go of our insistent, childish, self-seeking desires in order to find God's desire for us!

It is as we learn to submit our expectations to Jesus that we learn to identify our unique position and to discern between right and wrong desires. Then we have the discernment to claim rightly from the Lord that which he meant us to have now, in the last times, as well as that which he wants us to persevere in expecting from him at the end of time. 'Opening up' our expectations in this way is the way back from religious cynicism — it is as we learn to view our disappointed expectations through the eyes of Jesus that we realize God has not promised complete healing, now; he has not promised to take our responsibilities from us, here; he has not promised to renew this world, yet. But he has promised peace for our longing hearts, the peace of his kingdom which, on the one hand, *has* come and, on the other hand, *will* surely come, but only when it is ready, perfectly completed by the LORD himself. This way, you too could believe!

41

The Art of Waiting

Finally, something about the art of waiting, a lost art in our Western world. It is often our lack of appreciation for the art of waiting which lies at the heart of our disappointments. As modern and post-modern people we are so impatient. We experience waiting as a waste of time — that 'latest updated version' is always 'worth the investment' if it can only save us a few precious minutes! To us waiting is a disaster.

The Bible sees it differently. In biblical history, again and again we see how people had to learn to wait, through shame and loss. To wait properly is not a waste of time but an art! Abraham had to learn it, and Moses. And Jeremiah. Jeremiah even said, 'It is good to wait quietly for the salvation of the Lord' (La. 3:26). During times of waiting we suddenly find that it is not meaningless at all — it is necessary. Waiting *prepares* us for *receiving*. Yes, waiting is in effect allowing yourself to be given something. Of course it is difficult, because we are conditioned to go and grab it quickly for ourselves. Waiting is *not* giving up. It is reaching out with open hands to receive that which has been promised. In Hebrew the word for waiting is derived from the word for a string. When we read that 'it is good to wait quietly', it does not mean waiting passively, but, literally, tensed like a strung string, to look forward to receiving the promise. How amazing that in Hebrews 11 it says of all the believers under the old covenant that their most important work was this — that they kept 'looking ahead', 'looking forward', longing for the 'city with foundations, whose architect and builder is God'. They did not receive it, but they never gave up *actively* waiting for it. That is the art of waiting.

However, waiting is not only an art. A person who has never learned to wait, has also never grown up. We may think of waiting as an empty and useless waste of time. Waiting is boring. When we wait, nothing happens. But is it true that when you are suddenly forced to wait, nothing happens to you? On the contrary, much happens! All sorts of emotions rise up and stir inside you — irritation, a compulsive desire to do something, lost feelings of emptiness, boredom, longings — emotions you never knew were there. And suddenly it becomes clear that, like a child bribed with sweets, you have quietly been kept busy running in the rut of modern living by the superficial rewards of possessions, social position, leisure and entertainment . . . action-packed, constant need-fulfilment. When these are suddenly taken away you sink down into the emptiness inside yourself. That is why, at heart, waiting is to grow, to ripen, to mature — that which happens to the seed in the dark soil under the winter frost and snow . . .

God brings times of waiting upon us so that we might learn what is really important, come to recognize our idols for what they are, and adjust our future expectations: to look forward to *his* coming — now, and soon. Isaiah says that, 'Those who hope in (wait for) the Lord will renew their strength. They will soar on wings like eagles; they will run and not grow weary, they will walk and not be faint' (40:31).

43

Summary

Behind our inability to believe or trust there often hides deep disappointment. We need to learn how to deal with our disappointments in order to be released into trusting and intimate relationships. We might have adopted the same wrong strategies to cope with our interpersonal disappointments as with our disappointments with God.

It takes courage to handle our disappointments. But there are guidelines that point the way. If we handle our disappointments correctly we grow in maturity and intimacy; we also find the way back from religious cynicism to real hope for now and the future. Closely related to disappointment is the difficult but essential art of waiting.

Questions

1. Does waiting for something mean that I expect never to experience it for myself, simply shifting that which I long for to an indefinite future? Refer to Rom. 4:16-25; Acts 1:4; Jb 42:10-17.
2. Why is it so hard to acknowledge disappointment?

3. Can you think of an example of someone who felt disappointed in God — how did God finally answer them?

44 Bible Readings

Genesis 1:27, 45:25-28; Psalm 42, 139:23,24; Ecclesiastes 3:11; Lamentations 3; Isaiah 40:31; Matthew 6:33; 11:2-6; Luke 24; Galatians 6:2,4,5; Hebrews 11; 1 John 4:1; Revelation 21.

For Further Reading

Augustine, *Confessions*
Crabb, L. *Inside Out* (Amersham-on-the-Hill, Bucks: Scripture Press, 1988)
De Waal, E. *Seeking God* (Fount Paperbacks, 1984)
MacDonald, G. *Rebuilding your Broken World* (Highland Books, 1988)
Nouwen, H.J.M. *The Wounded Healer* (New York:Image, 1990)
Smith, H.W. *The God of all Comfort* (Moody Press, 1974)
Yancey, P. *Disappointment with God* (Marshall Pickering, 1988)

3

Anxiety – an Obstacle to Growth!?

Just as the occasional rumblings and clouds of vapour that escape from an active volcano give no indication of how much molten lava is building up pressure below, so too with our anxieties — they slumber deep down and show themselves only in sporadic, often unrelated outbursts. It is important to understand this secretive nature of anxiety, especially when you are surprised to find sudden, unexpected, strong negative feelings which make it impossible for you to believe.

Anxiety always robs us of our enjoyment of life; it shrinks our experience-field. It puts a damper on all we do and hurts us by infiltrating our most precious relationships.

Like disappointment, anxiety derails our ability to trust. Just as nobody will venture onto a frozen river or lake if there is any doubt whether the ice is thick enough, so nobody will entrust themselves to the people around them if they cannot be sure it is safe to do so. Anxiety arising from secret fears might keep you from coming to faith. If you are a believer anxiety might be stunting your growth towards maturity. In this chapter I will look at how a person can identify their anxieties; how to get rid of them, to control them instead of being controlled by them.

46 Identifying Anxiety

The first thing we notice about anxiety is its tendency to hide itself. It attacks in secret. Only rarely will anxiety announce itself at the front door and ask your permission to enter. It is no gentleman. It prefers to sneak in by the back door, invisible, and betraying its presence only by muffled sounds and faint odours. When you notice these it is time to go and find the culprit.

The symptoms of anxiety can be very diverse. One person rushes around in a whirl of activity, fleeing from rest and quiet, prayer and contemplation; another experiences exactly opposite symptoms and feels lethargic, low, and lacking in energy. One person talks incessantly and is always busy, yet somehow without making real contact; another is ultra-cautious, inhibited, and never ventures into the unknown.

Despite the diversity of symptoms, anxiety always results in superficial relationships and finally in self-alienation: the anxious person might even dislike themselves and lose their sense of identity. Anxiety often causes indecision and a person suffering anxiety struggles to make up their mind. They follow a zig-zag course in decision-making which drives everybody around them to despair. Anxiety has many manifestations but, as already pointed out, it always acts secretly — like an assassin, quietly, stealthily. It attacks one person with insecurity which leads to self-defensiveness and depression; another person, with pride leading to hard aggression; some people with over-confidence resulting in unrestrained behaviour; others with obsessive behaviour patterns leading to domineering, inflexible attitudes. Anxious people have trouble; ultimately they are heading for a crash but there are many stations before the final derailment.

However many stages there may be, it is always true that anxiety makes slaves of us. The Bible refers to slavery in Ga. 4:9 (slavery was a well-known New Testament phenomenon), but today the image of a robot or clone might be more appropriate — a stunted being, limited in its ability to relate and respond to others, nature, or God.

Psychological descriptions

A contemporary psychologist, Fritz Riemann, identified four basic kinds of anxiety which can affect all human beings. He linked each one to a question: a) Dare I be myself? b) Dare I give myself? c) Dare I change? d) Dare I belong?

These anxieties operate in polarized pairs and Riemann used the image of the solar system and the forces operating between the planets and the sun to describe the pairs. The first two anxieties he illustrated with the image of the earth as it circles the sun while, at the same time, turning around its own axis. People interact with each other while, simultaneously, keeping in conscious contact with their own inner selves. The second pair of anxieties

Riemann illustrated with the centripetal (gravity-seeking) and centrifugal (gravity-shunning) forces which keep planets in orbit around the sun. People need to be connected into relationships with others, while simultaneously keeping their distance and preserving their independence.

48

In her book, *Our Inner Conflicts,* Karen Horney similarly describes four anxieties. She links each one to a particular fear: a) fear of being exposed, b) fear of commitment, c) fear of losing control, and d) fear of failure.

It is obvious that her description matches that of Riemann. I will use a similar fourfold approach to describe the secret ways of anxiety in our lives:

a) Fear of becoming myself. To use Riemann's imagery, people who suffer from the first kind of anxiety circle around others but never turn on their own axes. They always show only one side of themselves. Their anxiety relates to a deep fear that they might not be able to cope when left to stand on their own feet.

I remember a conversation with a young mother after the birth of her first baby. Home alone during the day she felt very low though there was no reason for it. She had a lovely home. Her husband had a successful career and enjoyed his work. The baby was delightful. But the mother felt lost. As we talked on, I discovered that she had married very young. There were few opportunities to explore life and develop herself before her marriage and therefore she had no clear idea of her own identity. When I suggested that she should take up part-time studies, more resistances surfaced. First she objected that this would be too difficult. Then she objected that she would feel guilty at spending so much time on herself. Clearly, behind her objections was deep anxiety — what she most desired was also what she most feared.

Such anxiety may go back to a person's childhood. In this girl's home there had been limited encouragement for her as a child. Perhaps her family stressed the need to 'fit in', to be accommodating, not demanding, pleasing to others. There was a narrow band of acceptable behaviour and deviation from it put her in danger of rejection. The question in the heart of such a person is: 'Will I be rejected if I show who I really am — dare I be my*self*?'

A Christian upbringing can reinforce this anxiety if children are taught exclusively that God wants them to serve others, to lose themselves, to give up their own desires. Their fear of becoming themselves is strengthened further if it is added that God always sees them and has a little book in which he records all their mistakes. Unfortunately many Christians read the whole Bible in the light of Mt. 16:25: 'For whoever wants to save his life will lose it, but whoever loses his life for me will find it.' They interpret it to mean that you must hate your own life — that it is sinful to seek and discover who *you* are. If they never meet God in a different light, then, as far as they are concerned, it is God's will that they bear this anxiety — it has his divine stamp of approval.

But, on the contrary, the true meaning of the Bible is quite the opposite. Jesus puts his arm round the shoulders of every person and says: 'You are welcome just as you are. Please allow your life to radiate all that I have put into it!'

Yes, the Bible certainly speaks about a God who disciplines his children. But a good parent disciplines to affirm and not to destroy. A good parent disciplines to say, 'You are so valuable to me that I do not want to be indifferent and let that which is ugly in you pass unnoticed.' It is also expressed in the well-known saying that 'God hates sin but loves the sinner.' Because God so cares for each person, he does not want them to continue in that which makes them less than what they were created to be. Like a father he teaches and disciplines his children, trains them by discipline, not to discourage them but to educate them for life (Pr. 4, Heb. 12:5–11).

The Bible refers to this kind of anxiety in Ps. 107:10–15 and in the parable Jesus told in Matthew 25: 'So I was afraid and went out and hid your talent in the ground' (v. 25). There it affirms our individual uniqueness and encourages us to respond in affirmation so that we may find our reward from the LORD himself.

b) Fear of surrendering myself. Returning to Riemann's images we can describe people who suffer this kind of anxiety as people who turn on their own axes but never circle around others. Like an earth which turns on its own axis but has lost contact with the sun, its source of energy and life, they cannot be warmed, but die. This anxiety relates to a deep fear of belonging, of losing independence.

I remember a student who came to visit me. We talked for some time. Finally he confessed how desperately lonely he really felt. It is normal to suffer deep feelings of loneliness during the adjustment from secondary school to university. But five years later on he still felt that he did not belong to any group and had no intimate friends. He also told me that he had a deeply romantic relationship with nature and had strange eating habits. This person was hiding in an ivory tower with all the drawbridges safely pulled up. He experienced life as a kind of knight errant out on a lonely adventure — because it was not safe for him inside the community. But it brought him no joy; he felt only emptiness. After all, as human beings we have been designed for interpersonal relationships, as people-in-communion. Our relationships define us and give us roots. But the person who is anxious about joining in, belonging, putting themselves in a relationship which they experience as dangerous and which they fear might hurt and disappoint them, that person chooses isolation and a forced independence, instead.

This anxiety may have come from a person's childhood. Perhaps such a person had to learn to stand on their own feet quite early on because it was not safe in the community of their family. The question in their heart is: 'Will I be safe when I give myself to others? Or will they disappoint me, use me, abandon me?' Their anxiety makes them suspicious of everybody and every relationship.

It is possible that such anxiety can be reinforced by a spirituality which mainly emphasizes the holiness of God — for who can entrust himself to a God who is a consuming fire (Heb. 12:29)? It is very unhelpful to tell someone who suffers from this anxiety to 'trust in God' and 'commit' themselves to Jesus. They have learnt that it is dangerous to join, to lose freedom and become vulnerable, to open themselves up to disappointment. A call to surrender creates intense feelings of resistance in them. They will want to know: 'How can I be sure that God, or Christ, is different from all the rest? How can I be sure that I can trust God? Will it also end in disillusionment?'

52

The Bible refers to such anxiety in Ps. 116:11, 'In my dismay I said, "all men are liars".' And in *The Boundaries of our Being* the theologian Paul Tillich describes this anxiety as feeling like a small child in a big, bad world — be careful, your safety depends on your being suspicious! That is why the symptoms of this anxiety often include bizarre eating habits and all sorts of obsessive behaviour patterns. These people who look like impregnable towers of self-sufficiency live in fear — fear to surrender themselves. If their anxiety continues unrestrained, it could drive them into a private world of imaginary hallucinations.

But the Bible offers help to those who suffer this anxiety, and we can start helping them by accepting their inability to trust. They are victims of anxiety who need to know that they are welcome with us even when they dare not trust us. Behind their fear of trusting others they hide a deep desire to belong — that fear diminishes as they increase the desire! It is a profound biblical principle that a person receives more as they give of themselves. The good news is, 'Yes you will receive, as you give — do it!' That was also how Jesus invited his disciples to give themselves — 'Your reward will be many times as much' (Lk. 18:30). Ps. 107: 4–9 describes the relief that came to a fearful person who trusted God. Those people, who dare to give themselves, overcome their anxiety and change from being lonely and suspicious (Ps. 116:11) to becoming part of the joyful, celebrating crowd (Ps. 116:17–19).

c) Fear of changing. Some people dread a holiday in a foreign country, a change in occupation, a new liturgy in church, or changes in society at large. In answer to the question, 'Is there nothing that lasts?' they deeply suspect that, 'No, nothing remains the same' (Eccl. 3:20). They frantically try to safeguard themselves against all possible eventualities, even death, by taking out numerous insurance policies. They need to stay in control. Karen Horney calls this 'the fear of losing my equilibrium'; the fear of losing my inner balance. Such anxious people stick to that which is well-known, driven to seek only that which does not threaten them, always preferring the gravity of themselves and their own solid and predictable behaviour patterns.

53

Their anxiety may have originated in early childhood. Perhaps a chaotic family life forced such a child to create their own order and they found that a system of self-imposed rules helped them to control the chaos — as a result it became immensely important for them to stick to the rules; to stay in control became the highest priority of life. They are people who have to wash their car every Saturday morning — or tidy their whole house in a set sequence every day. But a family with order and, at the same time, space for freedom prevents this sort of anxiety.

This anxiety is mentioned in the Bible in Ps. 107:17–22. A religious upbringing can reinforce this anxiety — we see it clearly at work in the lives of the

Pharisees. They built a fence of numerous petty rules around God's commandments so that if they broke one of these they would still be safely within the boundaries of God's law! The fence clearly marked out the playing field — within it they felt secure and self-satisfied. But outside it life is dangerous: the unsafe, godless world had to be shunned at all costs. The Pharisees were certainly very religious, yet Jesus opposed them persistently for their preoccupation with the fence — which only obstructed their view of him (Jn. 5:39,40).

On the contrary, Paul, though he had been a Pharisee himself, instructs his friends 'You, my friends, were called to be free. But do not use your freedom to indulge the sinful nature; rather, serve one another in love' (Gal. 5:13). It is as we stop serving our anxiety and allow God to be in control that we can share his infectious freedom — 'infectious' because it might spread to those around us. To create relief we should ask these victims who fear change whether they realize how much they suffer under their rigid lifestyle. Is there not one little flower straining to bloom between the concrete slabs that order their life? Maybe one such flower will become the forerunner of the glorious springtime when God firmly and finally establishes his renewed creation. For them the good news is that they need not be anxious — it is not chaos that is coming, but a new creation! The true freedom of the Bible offers room enough to play and move safely within the boundaries.

d) Fear of order and rigidity. This fourth kind of anxiety stems from a fear of becoming stuck in a set pattern of life, in a rut, immobilized. People who suffer this anxiety are always on the move; they want to travel to faraway places. Riemann compares them to a world without the force of gravity — objects can fly away into space at any moment, controlled only by their centrifugal forces. Why do they so fear settling down? Because such people are afraid to fail. They cannot cope with the pressure of regular, daily demands and responsibilities. While they stay on the move they can always escape these and need not face their failures.

We read about them in Ps. 107:23–32 — people who sail the oceans and trade across the seas, always seeking adventures, never to be tied down. They need the stimulus of new and challenging experiences, movement, drama, noise, change. When they walk into a crowded room they immediately draw all attention to themselves. They are the heroes of the advertising industry! They feel stifled in a secure career with one partner and a family to be responsible for. They dread the feeling that they cannot escape from a situation. But these Don Juan types live in a world of fantasy. They are often deeply narcissistic and though they talk freely about their intimate and private emotions, one never experiences real intimacy with them. They are sometimes described as 'hysterical'.

This anxiety can have roots in early childhood. Such a person dreads becoming the 'failing helper'. It might be that their parent clung to them, the child, in order to cope with their own life. But a child can never adequately support their parent and is left, ever afterwards, to feel like a 'failing helper'. So deep is their fear of failure that they (subconsciously) decide never to get involved again.

Sometimes spoilt children suffer from this anxiety — for later in life they need to perform well, pass exams; it becomes harder to gain recognition. They become anxious about failure and prefer ever-changing relationships where they can sustain an appearance of strength. But their short and emotionally intense relationships do not really satisfy them. Behind their facade of independence they hide a deep longing for stability, acceptance, and freedom from the fear of failure.

A Christian upbringing which seems to tell us that *we* are responsible for saving the world, that *we* have been entrusted with the truth — as if we all have become little messiahs — can reinforce this fear of failure. It is possible to read the Bible and stay blind to the fact that the world *has* already been saved by Jesus, and that it *will* finally be saved only by him. No one else can save the world and no one has to. There is only one Messiah, one Mediator between God and the people, Jesus Christ, and he has saved the world, completely (Jn. 3:17).

Though this anxiety can be reinforced by religion, faith can also heal it. It is a good starting point to ask what it is that you really fear. Why are you afraid to be tied down? Is it disappointment you fear? In what or whom? Are you are afraid you might not be able to live up to expectations? And if you *do* fail, what then? Does every little failing make you feel as if you have failed totally and bring to mind that disappointed look on your parent's face? Does it fill you with guilt? In the gospel of John, Jesus said to his disciples: 'In the world you will have trouble (including anxiety). But take heart! I have overcome the world'

(16:33). He added, 'I have told you these things that in me you may have peace.'

A biblical description

To return to Riemann's imagery, it is only as a planet 57
circles other bodies that it can continue its elliptical course
— centrifugal and centripetal forces need to balance each
other to keep it in orbit. So, Riemann concludes, we as
people also need to be in relation to those around us and,
simultaneously, in touch with our own inner selves in
order to lead meaningful lives — we need to balance our
needs for attachment, belonging, detachment, and freedom. I agree with the conclusions of Riemann. I believe
that maturity is an achievement of dependence-in-independence. It involves a fine balance and can be illustrated
like this:

$$\text{myself} \quad \overset{X}{\underset{}{\longleftrightarrow}} \quad \overset{Y}{\underset{}{}} \quad \text{world outside}$$

If I move too far in the direction of X, I am too independent; if I move too
far in the direction of Y, I am too dependent. Ideally an ellipse with 'myself'
and 'world outside' as focal points describe the optimum course for my life. If
the foci move too close together along the imaginary line that joins them,
there is fear of becoming myself; if they move too far apart, there is fear of
giving myself.

But I miss a biblical perspective in Riemann's description. His images of interplanetary motion and universal
forces are helpful to illustrate the many confusing symptoms of anxiety, but they create the impression that life is
finally all about finding harmony and balance — that our

greatest need is to recover our lost equilibrium. New Age teaching responds readily to such a diagnosis and focuses attention on the process of achieving harmony. However, the Bible responds with a different diagnosis — and it prescribes not harmony, but therapy. The fallenness that makes victims of us all is more than just a loss of harmony and inner balance, though that is part of it. It is a fatal fallenness that affects all our relationships; a brokenness that needs healing.

As human beings we have not been created to be independent but to be meaningfully related to the lives of others around us — unlike the freely rotating atoms of an inert gas; more like the shared atoms in a metal. Within the network of inter-relationships each person longs to be recognized and appreciated — to be enjoyed, loved, guided, befriended, challenged, and included, with a smile and a friendly wink. At the very highest level each person has a deep longing to know also the all-encompassing meaning of our lives — that which makes sense of all of existence.

Creation. According to the Bible such a deep longing for interpersonal relationships was already felt by the first human beings when God created them to need regular food, drink, exercise, friendship, creativity, work, and intimacy — with a purpose. Ultimately the purpose was to be his image, to be the revelation of God himself in his creation. So our journey started with a clear destination. And along the way many longings fill us. We hear this in the first recorded poem:

At last, flesh of my flesh
bone of my bone
she shall be called woman
for she was taken out of man
        (Gn. 2:23)

It expresses the fulfilment of a deep longing. After having 59
waited and searched for a long time Adam meets Eve and
she suits him perfectly. He longs to be united with her and
become as one yet without losing uniqueness. It expresses
our universal longing to give ourselves, to contribute to
an intimate partnership, yet without losing ourselves and
becoming indistinct.

Fall. Immediately after this poem we read the poignant
story of the first disobedience. When Adam and Eve ate
the forbidden fruit they experienced the opposite of what
the serpent had promised — the serpent had said: 'When
you eat of it your eyes will be opened, and you will be like
God, knowing good and evil' (Gn. 3:5). But when they
ate it their first realization was not that they had become
like God — rather, that they were naked, 'naked apes'!
And it scared them. Desire turned into anxiety as they
tried to cover up their miserable nakedness with fig leaves.
And when God arrives in the early evening, calling
'Where are you?' the fearful reply is, 'I heard you in the
garden, and I was afraid because I was naked; so I hid.' On
all the previous days there had been a happy reunion
between Adam and Eve, and their Maker, but now there is
only fear. When desire became anxiety, fear and distrust
replaced spontaneity, openness, trust, and happiness.

It is not hard to understand why Adam was overcome by anxiety. He had distrusted God's intentions in forbidding the eating of that fruit; he had rejected God and preferred to trust the implied promises of the serpent. Now he feared God's rejection. Could this be *the* primary anxiety, the 'ancestor' of all our anxieties — the fear of ultimate, final rejection by our Maker?

Many forms of anxiety developed out of the distrust that entered life in Genesis 3 — it displaced longing with fear; self-confidence with self-rejection; and the rest of the Bible catalogues how anxiety works itself out in the fallenness of ordinary people. But the Bible is ultimately *good* news — it brings, also, a message of healing!

Bible case studies. Not only Adam, but also Abraham, Moses, Israel (Jacob), the disciples of Jesus, and even Jesus himself, were overcome by anxiety at times.

Abraham had just received the special promise of God's continual presence and blessing (Gn. 12:13), when he toppled from his pedestal — through anxiety. Because of a local famine he moves to Egypt but before crossing the border he says to his beautiful wife, Sarai, 'When the Egyptians see you . . . they will kill me . . . Say you are my sister.' He asks her to tell a 'white lie'. Why? Because of his distrust and fear for his personal safety (not to mention *her* safety).

Moses failed in Egypt, fled, and abandoned his vision for rescuing his people. When God calls him back to set the people of Israel free, he tries to get out of it by offering one excuse after another (Ex. 4:10,13). Why? Because of his deep fear of failure.

When God himself led the people of Israel out of the land of oppression to the promised land, they failed as a group because of anxiety. In Numbers 13 we read how the twelve spies reported their findings — a land where 'the people who live there are powerful, and the cities are fortified and very large' — they had even seen men descended from a giant race. Then we read that 'all the people of the community raised their voices and wept aloud'. They were so scared that they even wanted to return to Egypt, back into slavery and suffering. In the book of Joshua we read often that 'the heart of the people melted' (2:11; 5:1; 7:5; 14:8) because of a deep fear of being destroyed. It was a major theme in the lives of the Israelites — we could even call it the most important obstacle to Israel's conquest of the promised land.

It would take too long, as the letter to the Hebrews says (11:32), to tell of all the people who suffered and struggled because of fear and anxiety. The Psalms often express their cries of 'O Lord, I am afraid, be my safe place' (Ps. 25:17; 31:22; 38:21,22; 107:19; 120:1).

The Spirit of sonship. In the New Testament we also read, often between the lines, how people failed for fear. Think of Herod (Mt. 2:16). Why would he have murdered the baby boys of Bethlehem if he was not terrified by the threat to the safety of his own crown? Or the man who was possessed by an *evil spirit*. When he was confronted with the presence of Jesus he cried out in fear: 'Have you come to destroy us?' (Mk. 1:24). In the parable of the talents Jesus tells us that the servant entrusted with one talent buried his talent in the ground, for fear, because 'I

61

knew that you are a hard master, harvesting where you have not sown and gathering where you have not scattered seed. So I was afraid and went out and hid your talent in the ground' (Mt. 25:25).

Even the Apostle Peter, the very hero who pledged undying allegiance to Jesus, sank under the waves when anxiety overcame him — 'when he saw the wind, he was afraid and, beginning to sink, cried out "Lord, save me!"' (Mt. 14:30). Later on it was fear of suffering the same fate as his master that brought Peter to deny Jesus three times (Jn. 18).

Jesus himself experienced deep physical anxiety — the most extreme anxiety anyone ever faced. The New Testament writer records that 'he began to be sorrowful and troubled' in Gethsemane (Mt. 26:37–42), and prayed 'My Father, if it is possible, may this cup be taken from me.' Was it here that he faced that 'ancestor' of all our anxieties? Was it in our place that Jesus faced our primary fear of his Father's final rejection and the subsequent immeasureable loneliness, Godforsakenness . . .? In the letter to the Hebrews we read that 'During the days of Jesus' life on earth, he offered up prayers and petitions with loud cries and tears to the one who could save him from death, and he was heard.' (Literally, 'God answered his anguished cry', i.e. saved him from his fear!) 'Although he was a son, he learned obedience from what he suffered . . . and became the source of eternal salvation for all who obey him . . .' (Heb. 5:7–9). Hebrews emphasizes that Jesus came to save us from our fears.

In Heb. 2:15 we get the impression that God's great enemy uses anxiety to bind people and to prevent their full maturity — Satan uses fear to reduce people to slavery — and in the letter to the Romans our natural state as human beings is linked to 'fear' and 'slavery'. But in sharp contrast to such bondage Romans 8 promises sonship! Apparently there is a way to overcome the fear that makes us slaves — and it happens by the Spirit of sonship. This Spirit is freely given to each person who accepts Christ and it makes them respond, intuitively, with the cry: '*Abba*, Father.'

63

Seek Healing

I have shown that in dealing with anxiety it is not enough to seek to restore our equilibrium; therapy is needed for healing. Our fallenness is not just a loss of balance, though it is that as well. It is far worse — a severe disruption in the network of our inter-relationships which also disconnects us from our source of life, the Creator.

To me it is helpful to visualize the emotional life of every person as a finely woven piece of lacework, knitted without their consciousness throughout their early years. But during the process of life stitches are dropped, holes appear and the threads get tangled up, so that where love should have done the weaving selfishness took over, and instead of trust suspicion took shape. How can the lacework be repaired? It needs drastic treatment.

The marvel is that God not only created the world, but that he is committed to re-creating it. That is why he sent his Son — that we may be set free from the spirit of slavery, which binds us with the fear of death and judgment, and be put into the care of the Spirit of sonship (Rom. 8:15). The Spirit restores our confidence, openness, and the enjoyment of being ourselves, unafraid. It repairs the broken lacework of our emotional life significantly by restoring the severe damage caused by anxiety. How?

64

Multicoloured grace

Over and over again as I meet people I am struck by the many colours of God's healing grace (1 Pet. 4:10). For some people it takes the colour of a wholesome and deep affirmation, an encouragement to grow, to become themselves — which is what happened to Zaccheus the tax collector (Lk. 19). How wonderful that in the large crowd of people Jesus singled *him* out to talk to and accept without conditions! Jesus saw much in this little man who thought so lowly of himself and it is seen in the grace Jesus showed him — grace with the colour of unconditional acceptance.

For others that grace comes as a word of forgiveness — the very first words Jesus spoke to some were 'son, daughter, your sins are forgiven! You might think that what you have done is unforgivable and that you are doomed to become a wanderer like Cain, but you are mistaken — you have misjudged the grace of God.' This grace has the colour of an invitation to surrender themselves and be safe (Mk. 2:5).

Jesus sometimes set people free from obsessive and compulsive behaviour. Maybe they thought it impossible to shake off the restrictive rules of Sabbath-keeping in the belief that, 'this is what God wants of me — to keep his rules. If I keep them, no one can "get me".' But Jesus sees them as the captives they are and he confronts their legalism, breaks away the bars, and makes space for growth and movement. This grace has the colour of liberation and Jesus often challenged the Pharisees with it (Mk. 3:5; Jn. 3:3).

65

To others who are forever rushing along to change the world, to struggle against the current, Jesus says, 'Forget not that I *have* conquered the world. It is not you who have to do it. You cannot fail if you rely on me' (Jn. 16). This grace has the colour of a strong, supporting safety-net which can easily hold their full weight.

God's grace has many colours. It never runs out. It always encourages and surprises those who are without hope; sets them free or forms a safety-net, according to their need, individually tailored. It matches perfectly, every time. The only constant tint in this multicoloured grace is the golden thread which reconnects victims and sinners with their source of life, their Father, who will not rest until in love he has healed all his people.

Guidelines for handling anxiety

Are there things *we* can do to encourage God's grace in our lives, to help us fight anxiety and safeguard ourselves against it? Yes, and the following are some guidelines:

a) **Avoid treating symptoms.** Try to identify the secret ways by which anxiety enters *your* life. It is impossible to keep your doors locked all the time — dangerous too. But train yourself to notice its smell and pick up its sounds — talking it through with someone else; listen sensitively to others.

b) Go back to the longings. Always in extreme anxiety try to identify the deep longing it camouflages — for behind each anxiety there hides a longing. Those who long for intimacy fear it at the same time. And those who long to be themselves flee from becoming themselves. Behind the anxious need to be in control there often hides a longing for adventure and freedom; and behind the fear of belonging and stagnation there often hides a deep longing for security. It is only as we look behind the anxiety to find the longing, that God's grace, of a perfectly matched shade, can restore us.

c) Open up the secret passages. Deep-seated anxiety often causes subconscious resistances to faith. But what might happen when I open up the secret ways? I may discover that what I fear to believe is the counter-side of what I long to believe — I may fear and resist God because I long so deeply to find him. The Bible repeatedly reports people who 'did not believe it for joy and amazement' (Lk. 24:41; Gn. 45:26). We can be so scared of disappointment that we give up our desire instead.

d) Fight the anxiety in each other. It is said that the phrase 'Fear not' appears 365 times in the Bible — once for every day of the year. Usually these are the first words of greeting when God appears to people — 'Fear not, do not be afraid!' So we may confidently encourage one another, and ourselves, not to fear, but to fight anxiety. It helps to ask: 'What do you really fear?' — and, 'Are you anxious about *that*?' 'Can I give you hope that it might be different?'

e) Renew trust in God. Our deepest anxiety relates to our fear of God's ultimate, final rejection — there is no greater fear. And Jesus came to remove precisely this fear. He did it by going through it, removing its cause, and so becoming for us 'a source of eternal salvation' (Heb. 5:7–9). When we accept him we receive God's Spirit of sonship — who changes our life by reminding us, all the time, that underneath us are the eternal arms of the Father! (Dt. 33:27) There is no fear; we dare to become who we are, dare to give ourselves fearlessly; dare to enjoy change and variety; and dare to settle, attach ourselves and take up our responsibilities.

Wishful Thinking?

A person who suffers deep anxiety might well ask whether all this good news about substantial restoration is not just too conveniently matched to our needs. Do we believe it *because* it takes away our fears? Is that not just wishful thinking . . .?

No! I do not believe the gospel because it takes away my anxieties — I believe the gospel because, having heard it, I cannot deny or resist its truth. And when I accept it in faith it happens, as an added bonus, that it sets me free from my anxieties. That is a big difference. I will illustrate it from John's first letter. When John addresses fear (4:17,18) he does not say, 'Just trust in Jesus because he takes away your fear.' No, he refers back to how God acted in the Old Testament and kept his promises — God is the Creator and in him alone is light (ch.1), brokenness came about through the sin of people (ch. 2), God kept hold of humanity in love and sent his Son (ch. 3), and finally, God's love is shown not in our loving him first but in his loving us first (ch. 4)!

God's love is not a feeling; it is *solid*, made up of *deeds of love* which restored the freedom of his people. It is not a projected feeling of love; it is a matter of sober facts and history. John describes himself as an eyewitness to such history — 'have heard . . .have seen with our eyes . . . have looked at . . . our hands have touched' (1 Jn. 1:1–4). Without God's actions to back it up, the promise of restoration to freedom and joy indeed becomes only wishful thinking.

It is as you try it for yourself that you become convinced of the truth of the Bible. But if the Bible is right in its diagnosis, you have to accept its medicine too. In a restored relationship with God and with other people there is no anxiety, 'for fear has to do with punishment. The one who fears is not made perfect in love' (1 Jn. 4:18). Over against anxiety there stands love — and Christ's perfect love removed the judgement which prompts our deepest anxiety about death and chaos. Let the perfect love of Christ mend you — it is not *true* because it *works*, but it *works* because it is *true*!

Finally, to return to the title of this chapter — is anxiety an obstacle to our growth? Would it be a greater blessing if you could bolt your life against all fear and anxiety? Or have you been amazed to discover that anxiety can become a blessing and a benefit! Is it not a blessing that you feel afraid when you step onto thin ice? Or that you become scared in a dark forest? It stimulates you to protect yourself! It is good to be a bit anxious when you start a new job — it stimulates you to be accurate. Fear of failure at school might stimulate you to achieve good results. And fear of the judgment of the God of heaven and earth may stimulate you to seek him and be saved. Anxiety, an obstacle to growth ! ? Unfortunately it often is! Yet, at the same time this is not necessarily so. Brought into the daylight, stripped of its destructive power and put to good use, anxiety stimulates, protects, and encourages life (Is. 8:13).

Summary

Anxiety can present itself by many different symptoms in our lives. These are discussed with reference to the descriptions by the psychologists F. Riemann and Karen Horney. They identified two pairs of polarized fears: the first pair relates to the fear of becoming myself (independence) and of giving myself (dependence); the second pair relates to an obsessive fear of change (inhibition) and a hysterical fear of stagnation (Don Juan types). These fears often have roots in our childhood experiences and can be reinforced by biased or one-sided religious emphases. A biblical perspective sees anxiety rooted in our fatal fall-enness; we need healing, and not just the regaining of our equilibrium, our inner balance, our harmony. The most basic anxiety is our fear of God's final rejection. Behind our anxieties there often hide deep, hidden longings. God's multicoloured grace has a tint to match every kind of anxiety — it sets us free from the destructive effects of fear in our lives and significantly restores our relationships. As we experience God's grace it convinces us of the truth of the gospel.

70

Questions

1. Anxiety blocks our trust. Can this be inverted so that trust blocks anxiety?
2. Can anxiety ever be positive? If so, when?
3. 'He offered up prayers and petitions with loud cries and tears to the one who could save him from death, and he was heard (and saved out of his fear) . . .' (Heb. 5:7). Whom does this speak about? Who saved him? How and from what? (cf. Ps. 107:6)

Bible Readings

Genesis 2:23; 3; 12:13; 45:26; Exodus 4:10,13; Numbers 13; Deuter-onomy 33:27; Joshua 2:11; 5:1; 7:5; 14:8; Psalm 25; 31; 38; 107; 116; 120; Proverbs 4; Ecclesiastes 2; Matthew 2; 14; 16:25; 25:25; 26; Mark 1:24; 2:5; 3:5; 14; Luke 18; 19; 24:41; John 3:3; 5:39,40; 16; 18; Romans 8; Galatians 4:9; 5:13; Hebrews 12:5–11,29; 11:32; 1 Peter 4:10; 1 John 4:17,18.

For Reference and Further Reading

Crabb, L. *The Silence of Adam* (Grand Rapids, MI: Zondervan Publishing House)

—— *Finding God* (Grand Rapids, MI: Zondervan Publishing House, 1993)

Horney, K. *Our Inner Conflicts* (Horton, 1966)

Johnson, D. and VanVonderen J. *The Subtle Power of Spiritual Abuse* (Bethany House, 1991)

Lloyd-Jones, M. *Spiritual Depression* (London: Pickering & Inglis, 1976)

Nouwen, H. *Lifesigns* (New York: Doubleday, 1993)

Riemann, F. *Grundformen den Angst* (München: J. Pfeiffer Verlag, 1972)

Tillich, P. *The Boundaries of our Being* (New York: Fontana, 1966)

Zijlstra W. *Op zoek naar een nieuwe horizon* (Nijkerk: Callenbach, 1989)

4
Guilt or Shame

Some people find it easy to trust the gospel when they first hear it; it is good news to them. They repent of their sins and *know* that they are forgiven by God. But they continue to *feel* vaguely guilty. If they cannot get rid of those vague feelings of guilt they stagnate in their faith and finally conclude: 'I've tried to believe but it simply doesn't work for me. If only I could believe!'

A persistent feeling of guilt can be a pre-monition (a subconscious 'pre-feeling') which colours all our experiences and keeps us emotionally immature — immature also in our faith. When a good friend of mine first described maturity as 'being at ease with myself' — at home with myself, comfortable with myself — I thought it was a simplistic definition. But as I continued to mull it over, I discovered that his definition was, indeed, very profound. So many feelings prevent us from feeling at ease with ourselves. Have you ever returned from a discussion, a Bible study, an evening with friends or family and, as you are about to fall asleep, you remember incidents from your time together and think 'Oh no, I forgot to speak to so-and-so!', 'I should *never* have said that', 'Why did I not respond to his remark?', 'I wish I had been less sharp in answering her'? Most people experience such feelings of hindsight as a normal part of life, of their own imperfection and failure — they would have liked to have been different, but they're not. Some people, however, experience such feelings of hindsight with an intense and painful 73 sense of having failed again, fallen short. They feel guilty, ashamed, and ill at ease with themselves.

The Christian faith can reinforce such feelings of failure — for does the Bible not set an absolute standard? And who can truly achieve it? Even the Bible itself teaches us that no one *can* keep the law perfectly — still, the law is held up with holy authority and we are commanded to be perfect. No wonder that many believers are left with mixed feelings of impotence and guilt. What causes these feelings? Is there a way to be freed from such persistent, vague feelings of guilt? To answer such questions I have relied on the insights of Dick Keyes in his book *Beyond Identity* and used it as the basis for this chapter.

Guilt feelings often relate not to guilt but to shame

Just think for a moment about those typical feelings of hindsight I have described above. Analyse them and try to link each accusation to a corresponding commandment or law which has been breached — as David could link his guilt about Bathsheba to his trespassing of God's laws against adultery and murder (2 Sa. 12:13) — *in nine cases out of ten you will find it impossible!* For you did not steal, lie, or even covet; you did not, from an objective point of view, harm anyone; no objective commandment was breached to give rise to your feelings of guilt. If you had to go to your friends, family, or neighbour and confess your 'sin', they would be completely surprised and reply, 'Oh, we never noticed', 'Don't think about it — you were quite right', 'Forget it, you are far too sensitive.' How is it possible that a person can feel so intensely guilt-ridden when there is no objective reason for it? The Bible calls it shame!

74

Between East and West

In 1946 the American social philosopher Ruth Benedict published *The Chrysanthemum and the Sword* in which she analysed the subtle differences between Eastern and Western cultures. She called Eastern cultures 'shame-cultures' — traditional Arabian, Indian, and Chinese cultures — but Western culture she called a 'guilt-culture'. In the East there is no worse ordeal for a person than to 'lose face'; in the West the worst ordeal is to be 'caught in the act', found guilty of a public offence.

I agree with her analysis which is still largely accurate. Some years ago we had an Egyptian visitor to the L'Abri commune at Eck-en-Wiel. We were busy with building repairs at the time and all the guests helped along. We asked our Egyptian friend to join us and to help cleaning up some bricks by chipping off the old cement. He worked hard all afternoon without saying a word. But the next day he disappeared before we even started. Only much later we heard how deeply humiliated and hurt he had felt, how he had experienced the manual labour as an insult — and, as it was the worst kind of humiliation in his Eastern culture to lose face in front of strangers, he felt he had lost all honour and had to leave quietly.

Our Western world is very different. It revolves around (maybe I should say *formerly revolved* around) guilt and righteousness, justice and conscience. There is no worse ordeal than to be caught publicly in the act of breaking a rule — being found guilty. 'How can I find a gracious God?' was the question which motivated Luther to struggle for what became a new era in Western civilization. More recently the media has used our sense of justice and guilt to great advantage and 'being caught in the act' is still a powerful threat to every person in a position of authority or power!

What concerns me is that Western culture today is changing rapidly from a guilt-culture to a shame-culture: from the fear of being found guilty and facing punishment and humiliation to the fear of failure, falling short, losing 'street cred.' The combined efforts of marketing and media have greatly speeded up this shift. Whereas righteousness or rightness used to be central in Western thinking, it shifted to *perceived* righteousness or rightness. Today there are not many people who care deeply about real guilt — forgiveness has become largely a meaningless concept. But most people regularly experience a deep sense of shame — of falling short of the ideal, not making it, not feeling worthwhile as persons. Their shame becomes a barrier between them and others — and the more alienated they feel, the more ashamed they become. Shame also becomes a barrier between them and God — for however much he forgives them, they continue to feel less than ideal, not good enough, ashamed, guilty. This sense of 'guilt' has nothing to do with real sin and conviction of sin. It has everything to do with shame and failing to live up to that ideal image in our mind.

76

Is there a way out?

Is there healing available? Yes, but the medicine needs to match the disease. There is unique treatment available for guilt and shame respectively — but they cannot be treated interchangeably. There is a way out of the oppression of feeling forever guilty and inadequate — but the therapy that the Bible prescribes for guilt is quite different from the therapy it prescribes for shame.

Many people have never realized that this is so. When they feel guilty they intuitively pray to God for forgiveness. If their guilt feeling was in reality a feeling of shame, however, they cannot be forgiven and they rightly continue to feel guilty — in just the same way as people who drink cough medicine to relieve their arthritis do not improve their condition. Indeed, faith then works against healing and their feelings of guilt might even increase through such prayer. So what are the ways of healing that the Bible prescribes for guilt and shame respectively?

The amazing thing about the Bible is that it is neither Western nor Eastern. Just as Jerusalem is in the middle, neither in the East nor in the West, so the gospel speaks to both guilt- and shame-cultures.

Biblical therapy for guilt

When I feel uneasy and guilty it is important first to identify whether my feeling results from real guilt or whether, in fact, it results from shame. Guilt is moral — it concerns right and wrong, a command or law which has been broken or ignored. Guilt always involves the breach of a rule, law or commandment outside ourselves.

There are three steps in dealing with real guilt: the offender has to *recognize* that they have breached a rule; *confess* their offence; and be restored by paying the *penalty*. In a civil court a suitable punishment or fine will be the means to restore the offender. It removes their fear of punishment, for once punished they cannot be punished a second time for the same offence. When they have paid the fine they are free to go, and to forget about their offence. When we confess our sin or trespass to God, he promises immediate and total forgiveness, based on the fact that Jesus Christ has paid the penalty on our behalf. Sometimes we still have to bear the scars left by our sin, but the guilt is completely removed. The following diagram illustrates it:

guilt results from violation of law → repentance → forgiveness

Let's see how David, as 'a man after God's own heart', dealt with his real guilt. After his adultery with Bathsheba (2 Sa. 12) it took a prophet such as Nathan to quicken his conscience. But once David recognized his guilt he was filled with deep, sincere and intense regret. He confessed his sin to God and found forgiveness (Ps. 32; 51) so that he no longer carried any guilt — though the sin did leave him scarred. A contemporary Christian songwriter has expressed it like this:

78

> *The price is paid: come let us enter in*
> *to all that Jesus died to make our own.*
> *For every sin more than enough he gave,*
> *and bought our freedom from each guilty stain*
> (Graham Kendrick, M.P. 663)

Sometimes Christians continue to have feelings of guilt related to real trespasses they committed. They know that God has forgiven them but find his unconditional forgiveness impossible to accept. They cannot believe that Jesus has really paid adequately for them and feel they need to *add* to his payment. This may be as a result of their experience in the world where an offender's punishment or fine can never really repay the victim or restore the damage done. Such people need to know Jesus better. Alternatively, they might be too *proud* to receive forgiveness freely. They need to feel that they have contributed towards their own forgiveness. It interferes with their ideal self-image to think that they are helpless in earning their own forgiveness . . . it implies losing face . . . it is not real guilt, and leads me on to . . . shame!

Biblical therapy for shame

You might have expected the Bible to deal with sin and guilt, but you may be surprised to find that it also has a remedy for shame. Did you know that 15 of the 150

Psalms deal with shame — and that the word 'to be ashamed' is used 127 times in the Old Testament alone?

First, what is shame? Shame can be *positive*. It can be pure, like a secret covering, like the act of love in which Shem and Japheth covered their aged father, Noah, when they discovered him naked and exposed in drunkenness. It says they covered his body with a cloak, 'their faces turned the other way' (Gn. 9:23). Their brother Ham was without shame; but that brought him no honour, only a curse. Today there are 'de-shaming' clinics in Sweden — to desensitize people to their (healthy) shame. But to be shameless is no virtue in itself.

Although shame can be pure and good, the Bible shows it as *perverted* by the fall; it became a destructive force in our personality development; it drives a wedge between my real self and my ideal self: as I see my real self incapable of measuring up to my ideal self, I become ashamed and reject myself. Shame also drives a wedge between myself and those around me. The story in Gn. 3:7,8 describes how it started when 'they realized they were naked . . . made coverings for themselves . . . and they hid from the Lord God'. Shame entered Adam and Eve as they saw themselves in their pitiful nakedness and became dissatisfied because they did not measure up to their ideal self (as suggested by the serpent). They rejected themselves. Shame also entered the relationship between Adam and Eve — in their shame they found coverings to separate them further from each other. Then shame entered the relationship between Adam and Eve, and God — they hid from God out of real guilt and fear of punishment, but also out of shame for their nakedness.

Shame always involves falling short of that subjective, ideal self-image which lives in my mind — I am disappointed with myself and feel worthless. But how can falling short of an image in my mind cause such deep feelings of inadequacy and failure? And how does it come to parade itself as guilt?

At the root of shame is always a *distorted* self-image. Just as the image based on the lies of the serpent replaced the image Adam and Eve had of themselves based on the promises of God, so it still happens in this fallen world that people consciously or subconsciously construct totally unrealistic ideal images for themselves. We do not need much psychology to notice the far-reaching influences of 'Baywatch' and 'Gladiators', or *Ideal Homes* and *Top Gear* on the way we value ourselves. A deep sense of failure and shame overwhelms us when we have to face our imperfect teeth, acne or bald patches; our city-centre terraced house without front garden, or A–reg Skoda . . . It is obvious that the media have a powerful influence on our ideal self-images. It is not so obvious what causes a woman to feel vaguely guilty if she cannot do everything exactly as efficiently as her mother used to. If she thinks of her mother as a godly Christian woman, she might even feel she has disappointed God every time she fails to be just like her!

It is becoming obvious why the therapy for guilt cannot heal our shame: there is no breaching of an objective command underlying our shame, no sin to confess. Shame results from failing to meet deeply personal, subjective, and secret expectations of oneself. Confessing a person's self-image does not take away the fact of their failing.

They can try to hide from it. But that only alienates them from themselves, others, and from God; and the more alienated they become, the more inadequate they feel; the more 'guilty', ashamed.

The good news is that it is possible to be healed from shame. The first step towards healing is to stop hiding *from*, and go and hide *with* — find someone whom you can trust enough to go and hide with them *in* your shame, that you may be restored. Ultimately it is only God who provides such a safe hiding place for us. What happens when we hide with him? He accepts us as we really are. He teaches us how to accept ourselves in the same way as he accepts us. And he patiently teaches us to set realistic expectations of ourselves which will not lead to disappointment. The following diagram illustrates it:

shame results from failing my ideal self → hiding/acceptance

→ adjustment of self-image

Let's look at David again. He was ashamed of himself after he had fled to Ziklag and joined the Philistine army (1 Sa. 30:6) — while they were out on a raid all the wives, livestock and belongings of David and his men were looted. In his disappointment he turned to the Lord and found acceptance there which empowered him to overcome his shame and sense of failing — 'In you, O Lord, I have taken refuge; let me never be put to shame' (Ps. 31). It is in sharp contrast to Michal, the proud daughter of Saul who was ashamed when she saw a threat to her ideal self-image in David's behaviour (2 Sa.

6:20–23) when the ark of the LORD was brought into Jerusalem. She despised David, the LORD's anointed king and ended up under God's judgment for her real guilt in relation to a real trespass — a warning to us of the seriousness of not dealing with our (distorted) self-images. But the person who has found healing by hiding with God, can join in the song:

82

> Such love, pure as the whitest snow;
> such love weeps for the shame I know;
> such love, paying the debt I owe;
> O Jesus, such love.
> (Graham Kendrick, M.P. 619)

Redeeming my self-image. When we hide with God in our shame, we put him in an awkward position if we ask for forgiveness, because there is no trespass to forgive. Our shame is the result of failing to achieve our own subjective, fallen, ideal self-image. What repentance does for our guilt, exposing our self-image does for our shame. The final step in our healing from shame is to cleanse our self-images of the opinions of other people, the images from the media, even the images of saintly human role-models. Instead, adjust your self-image in accordance with God's promise, what *he* is achieving in your life and what *he* has gifted you to be.

The self-image you receive from God will reflect his character. God always works personally — he does not expect the same from everyone. He knows our weaknesses; he understands our failings. He encourages us, shapes and forms our circumstances, and he never abandons us. Wherever the Lord is at work, he creates originals

— not carbon-copies or clones. Like flowers that show their most brilliant colours when they open up to the sun, we radiate our unique beauty when we allow the Holy Spirit to shine on us. He uniquely shapes some to become an ear for his body and others to become an eye; each one receives a place, and the eye is not given the impossible task of hearing nor the ear of seeing (1 Cor. 12). It is in that unique place that we find our purpose, our sense of unity with others — the very opposite of shame — and are left to marvel at how cleverly God has designed it all.

There are four practical guidelines for setting a healthy and realistic self-image:

• *Do not model your self-image on the stars of Hollywood, but on the star of Jerusalem.* 'Let us fix our eyes on Jesus' (Heb. 12:2) instead of trying to live up to other people. Not even gifted Christian leaders should be the models for your self-image. Paul pushed aside all the heroes he could have aspired to from his Jewish background, to follow only Jesus. He speaks autobiographically in Phi. 3:8,9 when he 'considers them rubbish' in comparison to the 'surpassing greatness' of Jesus Christ, his role model.

• *Accept yourself.* In one therapy technique all partakers learn to pray, 'Lord give me the will to accept what I cannot change, the courage to work at what I can change, and the wisdom to know the difference between the two.' We are fallen; we live in a fallen world; and we therefore are not what we should be.

• *Build on what you have achieved.* Build up a realistic and healthy self-respect by learning from your past mistakes and building on your successes. It always reminds me of the famous inventor Edison. When he was looking for a filament which would be able to glow for more than a few seconds in his newly invented lightbulb, an assistant asked him if they should not abandon the project after having unsuccessfully tested threads of more than a hundred different compounds. Edison replied, 'We have found, so far, at least 100 compounds with excellent resistance to electricity'!

84

- *Choose your friends wisely.* We need mirrors to help us see what we look like. That is what the community we live in can do for us. Ideally we communicate with friends who can speak the truth in love. 'Iron sharpens iron' (Pr. 27:17) — sometimes it makes the sparks fly, but the result is a better, sharper instrument. The Christian community should be like this, a community where people do not just say what others want to hear, in order to please their own egos, but where people speak honestly, and in love shape each other to become more Christ-centred. Ultimately such creative communication should be most perfectly seen in Christian marriages, *the* human relationship with greatest potential to image the intimacy we have with God himself (Eph. 5:32).

Art or kitsch

Have you ever watched the T.V. programme 'Antiques Roadshow'? People bring along all sorts of objects — a vase, an old clock, a music box, old plates, jugs and ornaments — which the team of experts examine and value. What strikes me again and again is how my feelings can change towards an object. I may notice a vase. It has a nice shape, but it is not *that* special. However, when I suddenly hear it is worth £200,000 I look at it quite differently. It is not to my credit that I have to confess how often I discover the true quality of the vase only when I know its price!

This example helps us to understand an important biblical principle. Each person is unique and very valuable to God — he has given his Son for them. It gives each one of us a very astonishing price tag: 'You must know', says the apostle Peter, 'at what price you have been bought, not just silver and gold . . . much more . . . the precious blood of Christ' (1 Pet. 1:19). With this in mind we should look at others in a new way (as I looked at the vase in a new way), see them in the light of their true, infinitely great value.

85

Again and again I am encouraged by the good news of John, 'How great is the love the Father has lavished on us, that we should be called children of God! And that is what we are!' (1 Jn. 3:1). It gives me the energy to love others and myself, even when at first sight we seem to be only ordinary 'vases'. That the vase was so valuable is what changed my attitude to it. It also changed the way in which I would handle it — more in line with its true, precious value!

Restoration

Jesus told a most moving story of guilt, shame, and restoration in his parable of the lost son (Lk. 15). Having hurt his father, wasted his inheritance, sinned and lost face, the younger son finally returns to his waiting father and says two things. The first expresses his guilt: 'Father, I have sinned against heaven and against you.' The second expresses his shame: 'I am no longer worthy to be called your son.'

But the father is so happy at the return of his son that he sweeps aside the guilt with a grand gesture of forgiveness and puts his arm around his boy. The son's shame is taken away when the father accepts him back and calls out, 'Quick! Bring the best robe and put it on him. Put a ring on his finger and sandals on his feet . . . Let us have a feast and celebrate. For this son of mine was dead and is alive again; he was lost and is found.' The ring was the symbol of sonship. It showed everyone that his son was not only forgiven but also restored in honour, accepted back as a true son, his identity affirmed. The father puts his arm around the boy and says 'I am so happy that you are here again.' Without the second act of loving acceptance, the son would have been forgiven but he would never have lost his shame. He would have continued to feel that he had failed, that he had made a mess of it, had disappointed his father's expectations and his own hopes of himself — he would have despised himself.

The father's restoration of the son goes a step further than his forgiveness. When we receive God's forgiveness, he also goes further and it does not end as a legal formality but as a deeply personal restoration of our true identity.

Welcome

Many Christians experience God as the highest authority, far removed, with whom (if a person can present the right paperwork) there is forgiveness of guilt and a pardon for sin. But that is not the God and Father of Jesus Christ — he comes infinitely closer to us. Just think of Calvary where, in Christ, he identified himself with our deepest need. This is the basis for the hope we have, that we are safe with him and accepted. Ps. 31:21 says, 'In the shelter of your presence you hide them.' For each of us he becomes a Father who personally hides us in the secret place of his tent. There he says to each one of us, intimately, 'You may be ashamed about yourself, but I have no part in that shame — I am not ashamed of you' (Heb. 2:6, 11:16). Can you imagine that? A God who is proud of *all* his sons and daughters!

One evening we were discussing this very subject when I noticed how uneasy most people felt about it. They all knew that when we come before God at the end of time he will be concerned with judgement, grace and forgiveness. They never knew this other side of God, that he could possibly react like that and put his arms around us, wave aside all shame, and say, 'Welcome, I am proud of you!'

It is a theme which recurs in the Bible. In Matthew 25 Jesus told his disciples that at the end of time the Lord will say to them: 'Welcome . . . take your inheritance, the kingdom prepared for you . . . You have done well.' I detect a hint of 'I am proud of you!' in these words. Then Jesus imitates the surprise with which his followers will ask, 'But Lord, what have we done to earn this?' and replies, 'I needed clothes and you clothed me . . . I was in prison and you came to visit me.' In their low self-esteem, even shame, his disciples never realized how much their attitude to the poor and the naked had become like the attitude of their Master. By using Christ as their role-model they were aware only of their failure to match up to him. But God noticed their success. Sometimes our sense of failure is a lie to discourage us. It smells of that serpent-induced lie that first distorted our self-image. They *were* becoming the people God had intended them to be — though not perfectly and all the time — yet significantly and pleasing, acceptable to him. For you too it might be so on the last day!

Summary

It is very important to differentiate clearly between true guilt and shame when we experience persistent, vague guilt-feelings, because there are specific treatments for guilt and shame. To take the wrong medicine only increases our emotional confusion.

	guilt	shame
is	moral	psychological
originates from	commands	models
results in	offence/violation	distorted self-image
is healed by	forgiveness	acceptance
is concerned with	fear of punishment	fear of rejection
leads to	justification	glorification

The above is a summary of the characteristics of guilt and shame in our lives and of the treatment for each one.

Part of being healed from shame is to adjust our idealized self-images. As we see the astounding value God attaches to each one of us and take Christ as our role-model, we can be restored from guilt and shame to lead lives that please God and bring us great happiness.

Questions

1. Why is it so hard to differentiate between feelings of guilt and feelings of shame?
2. Is it a healthy sign that more people are today suffering from fear of failure than from fear of guilt? Why? Why not?
3. What are the origins of your ideal self-image?

Bible Readings

Genesis 3:8–10; 9:23; 1 Samuel 30:6; 2 Samuel 6:20–23; 12; Psalm 31; 32; 51; Proverbs 27:17; Matthew 25; Luke 15; Romans 15:7; 1 Corinthians 12; Ephesians 5:3; Philippians 3:8,9; Hebrews 2:6; 11:16; 12:2; 1 Peter 1:18,19; 1John 3:1.

For Reference and Further Reading

Benedict, R. *The Chrysanthemum and the Sword* (Boston: Greenword Press, 1946)

Keyes, D. 'Image and Reality in Society' and 'The Meaning of Shame and Guilt' in Barrs, J. et al. *What in the world is real?* (Champaign, Ill.: Communication Institute, 1982)

Keyes, D. *Beyond Identity* (Ann Harbor, Mich.: Servant Books, 1984)

Macaulay, R. *Being Human* (Carlisle: Paternoster, 1996)

Schaeffer, F.A. 'True Spirituality', *The Complete Works of Francis A. Schaeffer, Vol. 3: A Christian View of Spirituality* (Carlisle: Paternoster 1995)

5

The Journey of Life

A person's life cycle can be compared to a journey. The Bible also describes it like that — in Psalms there are repeated expressions such as 'the Lord knows the *way* of the righteous' (Ps. 1:6). It recently struck me again just how apt this comparison is — especially if we picture the journey along a minor road which twists and turns over fields, past farms, through valleys, over hilltops, along streams, and up steep mountain passes with breathtaking views and frightening descents.

I remember the road which connects the villages of Huémoz (where the Swiss L'Abri is situated) and lower-lying Ollon. It twists and turns between the two villages, over hills and through valleys, along rocky heights with beautiful views, hidden from the straight A-road which carries the noisy and polluting motor vehicles.

Around each corner you find new and interesting views; at every sharp bend you expect a dead-end. Often there are unmarked crossings and the person who takes a wrong turning here is bound to end up in a farmyard or on a rubbish tip. I think the writer of Psalm 18 had such a path in mind when he thanked God for the strength and guidance which had turned his path of life into a way of salvation . . . because it is possible to get lost along the path of life and never to arrive at the final destination. The hymnwriter, too, prays for God's help to find the way of life:

92

> *Teach me thy way O Lord*
> *Teach me thy way . . .*
> (M.P. 626)

In this chapter I will use the image of a journey to illustrate and explain the connection between faith, and the personal growth and development that all normal human beings have in common: from embryo to baby, from baby to toddler, from toddler to child, from child to adolescent, from adolescent to adult, and from adult to elderly person. I will concentrate on three aspects, namely *how faith operates* during each stage; the *relationship* between our faith and the stage at which we find ourselves along the path of life; and the value of a *timely word* for keeping us on track.

Stages of Life

Each stage of life is full of its own excitement and discoveries; also challenges and tests. Between the different stages we have to pass transitional phases and sometimes weaknesses that surface here will make us slip back into a previous stage. Psychology has brought to light many helpful insights specific to each stage of life. I adapted the following outline from the writings of the psychoanalyst Erik Ericson (*Identity, Youth and Crisis*, p. 94):

	phase	characterized by
i)	Baby (0–2)	basic trust – distrust
ii)	Toddler (2–3)	autonomy – shame
iii)	Childhood:	
	Play years (3–5)	initiative – guilt
	Primary school years (6–12)	capability – inferiority
	Youth years (12–18)	identity – confusion
iv)	Young adult (18–35)	intimacy – isolation
v)	Maturity (35–55)	generativity – stagnation
vi)	Age 60+	integration – disgust

There is a deep coherence between all the stages in a person's life and each person's journey has unique experiences and obstacles. But there are also common elements that we all typically share and which make interpersonal communication possible. For each individual there are twists and turns along the way — crises that test our skill and perseverance; continually changing views of the scenery — new perspectives we gain at each successive stage; and a final destination — for our lives are not just the product of chance and time but they have a goal which gives real meaning to the journey.

Faith and the Different Stages of Life

A journey implies motion. The journey of life is a constant movement from infancy towards maturity, a movement that leaves past things behind. At the same time there is always a new view coming up. In order to

persevere with the journey it is important to keep looking
forward with expectation, straining to get past the next
obstacle to the fresh view ahead. This is the incentive that
keeps you on track. That is why it is good to be aware of
what to expect of the future, as much as to take stock of
the past. I will use Ericson's outline as a basis for the
following discussion of the two-way relationship between
faith and the stage of life at which we find ourselves.

i) Basic trust — am I wanted?

There is a mystery surrounding the beginning of each life.
No one can fully understand how life is carefully and
secretly woven together inside the womb of the mother
— already possessing the full potential for all it might
bring forth in time. Psalm 139 says, 'You created my
inmost being; you knit me together in my mother's
womb. I praise you because I am fearfully and wonderfully
made.' This picture conveys a sense of trust; no one is the
product of a cold and mechanical battery cell or the
accidental cloning of stray molecules. No, there is a
personal touch behind each person; someone wanted you
to be here, behind and beyond your parents. Who is that
someone? It is the God of the covenant expressed in his
name, YAHWEH (LORD).

> O LORD, you have searched me
> and you know me . . .
> You hem me in — behind and before . . .
> Such knowledge is too wonderful for me,
> too lofty for me to attain.
>
> (Ps. 139)

This psalm of faith echoes the mystery which surrounds the origin of every life and its deep connectedness to the Source of all life. Ericson explained (*Identity, Youth and Crisis*, p.96) that 'basic trust' is built into a person during the very first stage of life. From the moment of birth a child receives the message, 'We are glad that you are here — you are welcome — you are small and vulnerable, but do not be afraid, we care for you.' The mother embodies it with her 'eyes that care' — giving attention; the father, with his 'guiding voice' — giving direction. Under ideal circumstances both parents will convey the message, 'It's all right — no one will harm you — do not fear.' In this way the parents, on behalf of God, weave basic trust into the life of their child. We can only understand what we've been given much later on when we leave our parents — their lives and teaching laid the first stepping stones for our own trust in God, the deep sense that, 'Though my father and mother forsake me (as in death), the LORD will receive me' (Ps. 27:10).

But not everyone experiences the early stages of life like this. If the mother never looked with 'eyes that care' the child might grow up to experience the eyes of God, also, as eyes that watch only to see when they do wrong. A child whose father's voice inspired fear instead of being a 'guiding voice' might experience God, too, as someone to fear rather than turn to. That is a particularly bad start to the journey of life. It is very hard to restore their basic trust later on in life — it takes special patience to cope with the recurring feelings of distrust, and a gift of grace from God's Spirit to keep them progressing on the path of life.

ii) Autonomy — giving and taking

During the next stage of life the child learns, literally and figuratively, to stand on its own feet and walk independently. Just as they will find it impossible to let go if they have not learnt that it is safe to trust their surroundings, so they also will find it impossible to obey if they have not learnt that those in authority over them are trustworthy. This stage can therefore be summarized by the word 'autonomy'. It is the stage for learning the important skills of giving and taking, obedience and independence, and includes being able to accept correction, warning, teaching, and help from others — for a person, though independent, never exists in isolation, but each person's independence is limited by the people around them. After basic trust, these are the next essential skills needed for progress along the path of life.

Under ideal circumstances, if a child has learnt basic trust during the first stage of life, they will now continue to grow into autonomy. They learn to give themselves to others but also to receive, and to operate within the space created for safe playing, within the rules of their family, and later on their school. They experience God's rules, too, as good, protective, and of benefit. Early on they learn to express themselves to God. He is the one who will not let them fall or embarrass them — 'Guide me in your truth and teach me, for you are God my Saviour, and my hope is in you all day long' (Ps. 25). God wants to protect us during this early stage of life — from failure, shame, and from feeling incompetent. He wants to do it through good parents, good brothers and sisters, good friends and teachers. But all too often this stage does not proceed smoothly either.

If roots of distrust have grown during the first stage of life, it will bear shame (which opposes autonomy) during this second stage. Shame causes a person to feel that they lack what is needed, that they are sure to fail. They dare not be independent or act with autonomy, for 'I'm not good enough, I'm sure to fail.' How can they ever get rid of those feelings of inferiority and shame? They may start with Psalm 25 and Psalm 86 which teach us about God's acceptance of us, even if we cannot achieve the standards needed to be accepted by other people — 'You are forgiving and good, O LORD, abounding in love to all who call to you' (Ps. 86:5).

97

iii) Identity — what suits me?

Adolescence follows next. Having learnt basic trust and how to give and take, a young person is now occupied with the question, 'Who am I really?' They discover an own inner life and a uniqueness they have never known before. During this stage of life all sorts of things are tried out to decide 'what suits me'. Is what my parents taught me really true and good? Can I defend it against criticism? On the one hand young people try to hide in their peer group — nothing is worse than being an outsider; on the other hand they seek to express their unique identity. The quest for their own self is central during this stage.

It speeds up a person's progress through this stage if they discover early on that there is a name which uniquely defines them: there is no other person exactly like you. In Isaiah 43:1 it says: 'But now, this is what the LORD says — he who created you, O Jacob, he who formed you, O Israel: "Fear not for I have redeemed you; I have summoned you by name; you are mine." ' God knows the names of all his children. And in the gospel stories, Jesus proved it by the unique way in which he encountered each person. Jesus was not limited by conventions or formalities. To him each person is a unique experience — he never treats us as 'just another number', just another one in the crowd (Jn. 10, Rev. 2:17).

iv) Intimacy — with whom may I safely share myself?

The next stage along the path of life is that of the young adult. The central issue during this stage is how to safely share one's uniqueness with others. How does a person find the right balance between independence from others and sharing involvement with them? This is the stage to enter into serious relationships and make far-reaching choices that will affect the rest of life — choices of a career, a life-partner, where to live, which church to attend. These choices are not made in a vacuum, but are squarely based on experiences from the previous stage(s) of seeking, experimenting, and discovering.

Under ideal conditions, if a person has learnt basic trust, giving and taking, and self-knowledge, he or she will experience this stage as a matter of course. This person will manage to settle and become attached — to discover intimacy. 'Intimacy' is therefore the keyword for this stage. As with a young tree which finally bears its first blossoms and fruit, this first fruit of life comes to one as a gift — as a reaping of that which has been sown in the previous stages. The gospel of John uses the same image (Jn. 15) and Jesus repeats, up to seven times: 'Remain in me . . . that you may bear much fruit.' That 'remaining in' the Lord is the condition for a fruitful life. It does not mean 'blending in' or losing identity — it means being totally myself and at the same time totally connected. Jesus defines remaining in him simply as 'doing my will', 'continuing in my love'. It is very personal, an attitude of dependence-in-independence, an attitude by which I look to God to work in me and at the same time roll up my sleeves and get stuck in myself.

v) Generativity — ability to nurture

In this, the most active and mature stage of the journey of life, the concepts 'settling' and 'care' are central. 'Generativity, then, is primarily the concern for establishing and guiding the next generation', says Ericson (ibid. p.138). A network of friends has been created, the family is settled and the children have been born. There are responsibilities in the church and community. Vital choices have been made and commitments entered into — longing has become caring. During this stage a person's relationship with God can be characterized as 'we are God's fellow-workers' (1 Cor. 3:9) — we might say, God's partners and, reverently speaking, his equals. I have come to know what to expect of the Lord, and I have come to know what God expects of me. We can work together to build up his kingdom and to cultivate and preserve his creation. We are partners, together. I am a human creature and God is divine, but we are bound together by one goal: to be creative providers and carers — for other people, the world, and creation — to portray God's covenant relationship.

100   The person who wants to be too *dependent* on God, struggles to bear fruit in this stage and stagnates. They experience other people as an unattainable standard to live up to, to try and please, or submit to. They destroy their own independence and creativity. On the other hand, the person who wants to be too *independent* of God, too autonomous, easily feels forsaken by God, as if they have to achieve everything themselves. They fall into a cramped and compulsive lifestyle and find it impossible to rely on anyone else.

The person who has not built up basic trust, who never learnt giving and taking, who never found their unique identity, and who has shied away from intimacy, faces the danger of becoming like a spoilt child during this stage — indeed they have never grown into maturity and forever need to be humoured and pampered. But the person who has grown into maturity through each of the previous stages of life can carry reponsibilities in a wide context, care for many different people, develop their unique talents, and store up an inheritance.

vi) Integration — looking back, how did it all fit together?

The keyword for the final stage of ageing is 'integration'. The central issue now is how to get a sense of peace about

all that has happened along the way. How do I look back
at my point of departure? And what is the destination I
look forward to reaching? Many people only now come to
accept some major experiences in their lives — 'so were
my parents . . . so are my children. . . that is what happened . . . that is what I had hoped to achieve . . .' They
can see the significance of each different stage better from
this vantage point and learn to accept the route their lives
have taken. Such a person has learnt to manage their
distrust, has come to know God and others intimately,
dares to be dependent-in-independence, and can sing
with John Newton:

101

> Through many dangers, toils and snares
> I have already come:
> 'Tis grace that brought me safe thus far,
> And grace will lead me home.
>   (M.P. 31)

But if a person fails in this stage — and it is infinitely sad
when that happens — then a disgust with life sets in; a
despair takes over which may have roots as far back as the
first stage of life. Paul did not see life like this. When,
towards the end of his life, he wrote to his spiritual son,
Timothy, he did not say 'I am glad it is finally over.' He
said, 'I have fought the good fight, I have finished the race,
I have kept the faith. Now there is in store for me the
crown of righteousness, which the Lord, the righteous
Judge, will award me' (2Tim. 4:7,8). Paul looks back at
what is behind, but he also looks forward to what is still to
come — the destination, the final reward!

Paul saw his life as a race. With such a perspective all of
life can be viewed as the earlier laps. Round the last bend

is the winning post, the destination of our journey, the city of which the LORD God himself is the builder and architect. To grow old with this in mind means to look back, not with self-satisfaction noting how well I have done, but with deep thankfulness experiencing all I have achieved as something given to me — accepting my failings and fallenness too as part of life. I can have peace with the fact that my path of life is coming to an end because I know that the Lord of Life is waiting for me at the finishing line — and he has prepared a unique place at his banquet for me and for every other finalist.

Yes, at the end of the path of life there is a *person* waiting. As each stage of the road rewarded you with unique and surprising views, each stage of the road also challenged and changed you. And so, along the path of life you developed into the unique person who will soon, at the end of the journey, receive a name from the Lord of Life himself, a name known only 'to him who receives it' (Rev. 2:17); a name which will satisfy, identify, and give infinite meaning to every stage of your journey of life.

When Faith goes off Track

What happens when the path of my spiritual development and the path of my emotional development don't run along parallel tracks? In the section above I have (mainly) assumed a journey of life where growth in faith keeps step with growth in maturity, individuality and personhood. That is how it should ideally be, but can a person grow into mature adulthood without growing mature in faith? To be honest: yes!

A person can develop into an emotionally balanced and mature person and still miss the image of Christ. However, such a person is not ready to arrive at the destination. Each stage of life has indeed developed as desired, yet they miss the depth-dimension which believers experience when they trust in God and have a mature relationship with him, the perspective and colour God adds to the views along the way. I believe it exerts an enormous pressure on the emotional well-being of a person to live with no goals beyond this world. They might find it increasingly *difficult* to let go of this material world — many people cling frantically to what they achieved, or deserved to achieve, or still wanted to achieve on this earth. Yet, in all honesty I have to say that there are others, *who* have no personal faith in God, *can* let go. Usually they are people who devoted their lives to goals beyond their own selfish interests.

On the other hand, a robust faith is not normally associated with an inhibited, stunted personality. Is it possible for an emotionally handicapped person to achieve spiritual maturity? What about the person who picked up basic distrust instead of basic trust, rule upon rule instead of order, inferiority and shame instead of confidence, loneliness instead of intimacy, and a disgust with life instead of integration? Can such a person ever become spiritually mature in Christ? I am convinced the answer is: yes!

The grace of God is big enough to deal significantly and substantially with people who have experienced deep emotional wounds. I know emotionally damaged people who *have* a genuine, trusting, and living faith in God, who can be described even as 'spiritually mature'. It is certainly not the rule and, sadly, more often the case that people *fail* to grow in faith because of the deep ruts left across their path of life by the roots of emotional damage. Often this kind of emotional immaturity underlies the agonized cry: 'If only I could believe!'

104

Real-life examples

This has been a very important discovery — that a person's stunted *emotional* development can be a real barrier to their becoming *spiritually* mature. It is a discovery that pastors, evangelists and counsellors do well to take note of. How often an evangelistic message includes the call: 'Give yourself in faith to Jesus Christ and he will rescue you from your troubles. He will forgive you and heal you!' This *is* the good news, but as I understand the gospels, Jesus always presented a call to faith in the context of a person's unique circumstances. Presented as a general call to faith it could leave many people shrugging their shoulders and ignoring the gospel with contempt because they experience it as irrelevant to their circumstances. Look at the following examples:

• What about the girl who was sexually *abused* in her family? For her the call to surrender herself to a Father is loaded with negative meaning. It equals rape. What she needs to hear, rather, is exactly the opposite: 'It is OK for you to be afraid of surrendering yourself — I understand — do not feel guilty about it.' She is deeply frustrated by the call to trust another person and to surrender herself to him, because her emotional development was impeded. She never learnt the healthy balance between intimacy and privacy. Perhaps she never learnt to say, 'I am a person in my own right with my own emotional life. I am not here only as an extension to fulfil the needs of others. I may reject their advances.' Believing is all about trusting. Such a disruption of trust during the early and adolescent years of life can deeply damage a person's ability to have faith. It would be better pastoral therapy to show her unconditional acceptance and so help her to discover that there *are* people who may be trusted not to abuse her privacy. Small steps of trust might pave the way to trust in God, who never forces himself into our lives.

• I believe that many disagreements within the *church community* can be traced back, essentially, to underlying personality differences; and some of these differences have led to painful and permanent schisms! Without trivializing the issues on which churches have divided (for some of those issues *were* of crucial importance), it is a fact that many divisions have resulted from individual, personal and emotional weaknesses.

• Take the problem of the *do's* and *don'ts* of church life: how should we behave on Sunday . . . and what about our liturgy . . . or the creeds which are hundreds of years old? Somebody who as a young child never learnt basic trust may grow up to find order in their life by frantically clinging to rule upon rule. God's law, too, they may experience as an iron rule. They strictly keep the Sabbath holy and expect others to do the same. Every change from that which is established, well-known, traditional, they experience as an enormous threat — for, 'What will

happen if we open up the floodgates?' As a child they may have had to obey implicitly or endure cruel punishment. If they came late for school or had an accident they felt ashamed. And now they forever feel guilty before God. They need to feel safe by protecting God's law with fences
106 to keep them from trespassing. Rather than reminding them that 'the Sabbath was made for people', they need to hear the words of Augustine: 'Love, and do as you like!' Dare to be human, dare to fail, for not every mistake leads to instant punishment and rejection. Of course not all changes are to be desired, but without change there is no life. Behind their legalistic mindset may hide a person who fears to be independent and prefers the image of God as big bogeyman to safeguard them from the dangerous business of personal responsibility, moving, growing, choosing.

The truth is that God offers us a safe play area — and when we fall, we fall into the arms of the God who is there. There is a song which expresses this in prayer:

> *So freely*
> *flows the endless love You give to me;*
> *So freely, not dependent on my part.*
> *As I am reaching out,*
> *reveal the love within your heart . . .*
> (Dave Bilbrough, M.P. 603)

It is in making mistakes, being weak and vulnerable, and still being *accepted* by others that a person grows emotionally — and might learn also to *live* (and change) in the presence of God who loves them personally and unconditionally.

A Timely Word

Finally, never underestimate the power of a personal word, spoken at the right time and in the right place, to save someone who is suffering deep emotional damage and hurt.

Each person's life follows a unique path — some are damaged during the early stages of the journey, others during adolesence. The stages of our journey are always intimately connected and weaknesses that we thought we had dealt with may resurface at a dangerous transition stage; old fears may trip us up along an unknown stretch of the road. It is important to have regular breaks, to look back and ahead, and to consult the map — we may find that we have taken a wrong turning three intersections back. You have a similar problem when you button up a shirt: if you have mismatched the first button and button-hole it may only show when you reach the last button. At this point there is nothing else to do but to unbutton all the way back. It can be tedious, especially if you are in a hurry, and it does not feel like progress at the time. The same is true of our handling of life; although it may not feel like progress at the time, sometimes to *return* to a past stage of the path is an essential part of recovery.

Maybe it is only at twenty-five years of age that you are able to handle that hurt which stems from when you were five — only at twenty-five you have the courage and insight to face the pain and find healing. I am not in favour of continually digging up the past but sometimes it is necessary in order to make progress. The French have a proverb for it — *reculer pour mieux sauter* — take a step back in order to jump further!

At such times an appropriate word of encouragement works miracles! Pr. 25:11 says: 'A word aptly spoken is like apples of gold in settings of silver.' This is how we should seek to pass on the message of God to others — not in a dull way, the same words for each person, but alive and suited to each unique situation. To speak the *right word* at the *right time*, that is the art!

To the person who is spoilt and headstrong, callously independent, one might say, 'What does a person gain if they conquer the whole world but lose their own soul?' Such a person needs to learn about intimacy, commitment and responsibility. But to the person who always denies themselves and serves others to gain their favour, one might say, 'What good is to the world around you if you deny them your*self* and your gifts?' They need to realize that true self-sacrifice would mean *not* denying themselves. The same applies to those who feel a compulsive need to spoil other people. They may therefore appear very humble but are really terrified of new experiences. Their behaviour masks their fear of being independent, of failing, of losing the approval of others.

To everyone who struggles with these problems I would say that God unmasks our motives — he sees our whole journey and can plot where we are. He has a fresh and appropriate gospel word for each person. Therefore seek him with all your heart. He has the first word and he has the last word; for every stage of your life he has a living word.

Summary

The life of each person is like a journey along a country road. At each new stage we experience new challenges and fresh views of the scenery. Psychologists have helped us to learn much about the unique characteristics of each stage of life. Looking at life in this way could create the impression that human life is a harmonious whole. But the opposite is true — it sometimes seems as if we have lost direction completely or are hopelessly handicapped. This also affects our faith. But God's word to each person is unique and suited to our individual needs, depending on the stage of life in which we find themselves. If God directs our journey, it changes our self-centred humanist mindset — for life always derives its meaning from the *person* who is waiting at the destination.

Questions

1. In Ch. 1 we said that believing is trusting. In this chapter we say that no person can mature properly without basic trust. How are the two related? What can we deduce from this about God the Creator's intention for us as people?

2. What is emotional maturity and when are you spiritually mature?

3. The medieval philosophers used to say that 'grace does not destroy nature, but fulfils it'. What do you think of this? Is it all that can be said about the work of grace?

Bible Readings

Psalm 1:6; 25; 27:10; 86; 139; Proverbs 25:11; Isaiah 43:1; John 10,15;
1 Corinthians 3:9; 2 Timothy 4:7,8; Revelation 2:17.

110

For Further Reading

Andriessen, H.C.I. *Spiritualiteit en Levensloop* (Apeldoorn: Altiote-
    Averbode, 1984)
Ericson, E. *Identity, Youth and Crisis* (New York: Norton, 1968)
Fowler, J.W. *Stages of Faith*, (Hansen, 1981)
—— *The psychology of Human Development and the Quest for Meaning*
    (San Francisco: Harper, 1981)
Sheriffs, D. *The Friendship of the Lord* (Carlisle: Paternoster Press,
    1996)
White, J. *Parents in Pain* (Leicester: IVP, 1979)

6

Suffering – the Danger of Despair

People sometimes find it impossible to believe as result of the deep despair that follows bereavement, suffering, or loss. 'Stop it! — every time I turn to him, it is as if I have the door banged in my face', Jack explodes in the film *Shadowlands* when the minister tries to comfort him after the loss of his wife. Every person who has experienced bereavement knows such moments when no word of comfort can pierce the darkness. The trauma shocks that which we know with our minds and it stuns our emotions.

Today there are many books and counselling aids available for those who suffer bereavement and loss — it is no longer necessary to be ignorant of their destructive effects. Religious doubts, denial, protest — these are all 'normal' stages in the process of learning to live again following bereavement. This chapter is concerned with the questions surrounding the meaning of suffering in our lives and what role God plays in it; the next chapter will deal more practically with the process of coping with suffering and how faith interacts with life in the aftermath of deep personal loss.

Why?

People who never considered themselves to be believers often spontaneously ask 'Why, God?' when faced with sudden, overwhelming suffering. Every religion and philosophy of life has its own answer to this question. However diverse the answers are, they add up to only a few possibilities.

If you are not very religious, suffering often leaves you with a deep sense of the tragic nature of life; you experience it as an endless cosmic struggle between good and bad — a struggle which is primarily chaotic and finally meaningless. Your suffering is therefore also meaningless.

Religious people tend to feel that, somehow or other, *God* is responsible. They might consider God as the single (*monos*) cause of everything — all things lead back to him. I will call this *monism*. But when they consider God as the one cause of both good and evil they ascribe to him that which is contrary to his holy character of light and love, moral purity and purity of actions. They *desecrate* God's name by taking away his holiness.

Alternatively religious people might see life as the result of an ongoing struggle between good and evil, between God and Satan. I will call this *dualism* — a view according to which two equal but opposite powers are locked in a struggle in which they sustain each other, in equilibrium. But if God is considered as one of two equal and opposite forces, God is made less than the unique, supreme being he is — God's name is *demeaned* by taking away his uniqueness.

John and Isaiah

The problem is that when we turn to Scripture to find an answer to our suffering, it seems to confuse us even more. It does not give us a definite answer; far from simplifying the issue it seems to lead us into an opposite direction!

The Bible seems to justify both the interpretations of monism and dualism and to illustrate it, I will quote Isaiah and John: '*I am the Lord, and there is no other. I form the light and create darkness, I bring prosperity and create disaster; I, the* LORD, *do all these things*', says Isaiah (45:6,7); '*God is light; in him there is no darkness at all*', says John in his first letter (1:5).

How should we make sense of these two statements alongside each other? It seems as if the one excludes the other, for Isaiah seems to desecrate God's name while John seems to demean it. If I could put a question to each of them I would ask John: 'If you say that God is light, without any darkness, what did Isaiah mean when he said that God is the creator of light *and* darkness, prosperity *and* disaster?' And I would ask Isaiah: 'If you say that God is the maker of light and darkness, good and evil, how can John say that in God there is *no* darkness? Whom should we believe — John or Isaiah?

Putting these two verses side by side reminds us that we should be careful how we read the Scriptures; it is easy, seeking a quick answer, to base our understanding on a single verse and conveniently to forget that there are other verses which might have a different slant. It is only as we seriously consider all aspects, including the contradictory ones, that we do justice to Scripture and genuinely learn from God. Facing two apparently contradictory ideas we often find a third way, a marvellously surprising way which reveals the majesty and authority of the God who does not fit snugly into our 'boxes'.

114   The right approach is to remember that behind both John and Isaiah stands the author of the Scriptures, the Holy Spirit, who has no ambiguous or confusing messages. So, what are we to make of the apparent contradiction between John and Isaiah?

Is God the Origin of Evil?

John wrote his letters as a warning to Christians in danger of being deceived by the 'gnostic teaching' of their day. It was very similar to the New Age teaching of today, namely that God is the one, all-encompassing totality in whom both good and evil have their being, one divine reality with two faces. So, after war there comes peace, after day comes night, invariably after death comes new birth.

This resembles the concept expressed by the image of Yin and Yang, the symbol used in many popular contemporary designs. It originated in the East where it is a common symbol of Buddhism and stands for the two opposite realities which seem to exist, inter-connected, in the world in which we live: light versus darkness; male versus female; death versus life.

Good and evil do not cancel each other out but rather complement each other — they are both necessary, as the plus and the minus sides of existence, causing at one moment terrible suffering (Auschwitz, 1940–45), invaria-

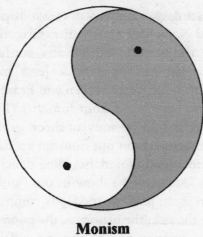

Monism

bly followed by positive restoration (the founding of the Jewish State of Israel, 1948). So all things work together for . . . equilibrium.

'God has a dayside and a nightside', says the main character in Graham Greene's novel *The Honorary Consul*. In this novel God is portrayed as having also a dark side, an evil side. Some orthodox Reformed churches promote a similar image of God by placing God's eternal election alongside his eternal rejection. Some even go so far as to say that inside God there is an eternal hatred alongside his eternal love — to me this idea seems quite close to the idea of Yin and Yang.

John states clearly that God is not the source or origin of evil, and that to suggest it would imply desecrating God's name. Rather, 'This is the message we have heard from him (Jesus) and declare to you: God is light; in him there is no darkness at all.' John's good news brings comfort: do not despair, for evil does not originate in the being of God. John does not write subjectively, based purely on his own personal experiences, but he writes on the basis of what he learnt from Jesus himself: 'We proclaim to you what we have seen and heard . . . This is

the message we have heard from him . . .' (1 Jn. 1:3–5). (Conversely we should be wary of theology that tries to climb up from below, from our human experience of evil and suffering to a level of understanding which it assumes is from God!) Jesus came to show us the Father, to make him known to us. In Jesus we see God's compassion for all who suffer — the sick, the prisoners, the poor. In Jesus we see God's deep aversion to evil, sin, and suffering. Death does not belong to life as the minus side of existence, as that which completes life. On the contrary, death is an enemy of life and destroys it. But Christ destroyed death!

In Jesus we see the one, unique God; he is not two-faced. He has no secret drawers. He is love and in him lives no eternal hatred. He hates the sin and death which has this world in its grip. But there is no Yin and Yang in God. John's message is not to have anything to do with such 'gnosticism'. In our contact with New Age teaching we too should not be swept along by it, for there is no harmony between light and darkness, truth and lies, love and hatred.

For there is an eternal separation between God and the dark source of evil. The person who thinks as a gnostic turns God into a devil and does not take evil seriously. Spinoza (1632–77), amongst others, taught such a philosophy — 'cognitio mali est cognitio imperfecta' — in which knowledge of evil is knowledge of the imperfect. In the same way as a child learns by burning their hand not to touch a hot stove again, suffering teaches us good principles and thereby evil is treated as being in reality good and wholesome. This thinking blurs the distinctions between good and evil and at present is influencing all Western thinking through issues as diverse as criminality, abortion, euthanasia (literally 'good death'!), nuclear armament, fraud, moral decadence. There is ever less separation between good and evil, right and wrong.

117

A god who needs good and evil to be complete is not the God of pure light. Thinking of God as having both light and darknesss within himself desecrates his name; the person who thinks of God like this needs to listen again, carefully, to the Apostle John.

Does evil exist outside God and outside his control?

If God is light and there is no darkness in him, do we therefore conclude that evil operates completely outside God? Does he have nothing to do with it, no control over it? Isaiah says that God made *both* light and darkness: 'I bring prosperity and create disaster.' It seems to contradict the words of John and, at first sight, might leave one to conclude: 'You see, it makes no sense; the Bible is a book full of mistakes and contradictions.' Though such contradictions in the Bible are not easily reconciled or understood, it is worthwhile stopping and examining them; they often illuminate an aspect of the mystery of God's being which is far beyond our human understanding.

If evil is not part of the being of God, does evil then exist as an equal but opposite force, not to be brought under God's control? Does dualism give an answer to our suffering? Is God one of two supreme powers — good and evil, God and Satan — interlocked and balanced so that now light, then darkness, has the upper hand?

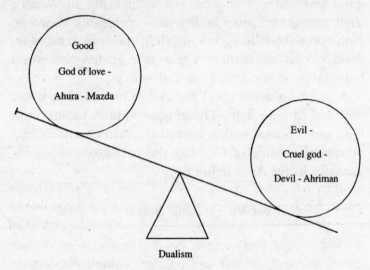

Good

God of love -

Ahura - Mazda

Evil -

Cruel god -

Devil - Ahriman

Dualism

Many people interpret Isaiah's prophecy against the background of dualistic thinking, which originated in Persia and spread to the Ancient East. They see history as the result of an eternal struggle between a good god and an evil *daimon*. From the origin of the world these two have been in opposition, controlling world history between them: first one, then the other has the upper hand, but there is no final victory for either. In this thinking there is no blurring of the borders between good and evil. However, whereas monism desecrates the name of God and takes away his holiness, dualism demeans the name of

God and takes away his uniqueness. If doom and darkness exist outside God, equally strong as he, then he is powerless against them. What hope do we have with such a powerless and pitiful God as our champion? How can he possibly guarantee victory over evil? Dualistic thinking gives great honour to Satan who would gladly be put up there, next to God. But soon the time will come when God will allow him not even the smallest pinhole in the universe!

Dualism might also have crept into the world-view of the Jews. They knew well that God was working through *them,* that God was good and almighty to *them.* But there existed a devil, the anti-God, who worked among the surrounding *heathen* nations. Whereas Israel, as God's people, were secure on the side of good, the surrounding nations belonged to Satan, the evil power. It is possible to read the description in Isaiah 45 of an eventful period of history in the context of this Jewish thinking. A new world leader would arise — Cyrus (Kores) the Persian ruler. He would do something absolutely amazing: he would allow the exiled Jews to return to their homeland and so would fulfil God's prophetic promises to the nation of Israel. Cyrus would be a political leader resembling Gorbachov in the Soviet Union or Mandela in South Africa in the one respect that, though not personally a believer, he would act as one would have expected of a believer. Isaiah responds to this and says, 'Do not think that this happens outside of the LORD. His hand is over all things.' God even calls Cyrus 'my anointed' (literally '*Messiah*'). That must have been a shock for the Jews. It is as if Isaiah was saying: 'Watch out with your separatist thinking. Yahweh is also Lord over non-Jewish kings like Cyrus. All world leaders are in his hand. Some he even calls to a mission of good works to bless the nations.' Thank God for all leaders such as Cyrus, and Gorbachov and Mandela! 'I am the LORD', says Isaiah as God's

120 mouthpiece to Cyrus, and he continues: '. . . whose right hand I take hold of . . . I will go before you . . . I will break down gates of bronze and cut through bars of iron.' The God of Israel is also the God who breaks down the Berlin Wall, and LORD of the world. He does all things for the sake of his plan of salvation (Is. 45:22–25).

Whereas John taught that 'there is no darkness in him at all', Isaiah says that 'there is no darkness apart from God'. It is no casual remark; it is the key to Isaiah's prophetic message. Isaiah precedes these words with, 'There is none besides me . . . I have created all things . . . I am the Lord, and there is no other.' God does not for one moment renounce full responsibility for his world. He alone is LORD of creation, LORD over the light and darkness, LORD over good and evil, the one who blesses and curses. Nothing happens outside of God — not the vast masses of people who have never heard of Jesus, not the endless poverty of the Third World, not the apparently meaningless drowning of a four-year old child or the secret loss of a foetus. Even if he is not the source of evil, evil cannot take anything away from his dominion. God is undaunted by evil — and *includes* it in his divine plan for salvation and blessing!

Dualism is very popular among contemporary post-modern thinkers who come to the despairing conclusion that good and evil, chaos and order, equally determine the course of history. They see no sign that things will ever change and experience life as deeply tragic; there is no possible victory over evil. The only choice left is between protest and resignation. But they need to listen again, carefully, to Isaiah, who reminds us that there is only one God who has all of reality in his power: 'I am the Lord and besides me is no other.' No balancing forces — no others!

The third way — evil in God's hand

To be faithful to the teaching of the whole Bible we need to resist both monism and dualism. Instead I believe we must hold on to two truths, simultaneously:

• *God's absolute goodness* — John shows us that we miss the point when we connect evil directly with God himself;

• *God's almighty power* — nothing escapes God, nothing falls outside his dominion.

Isaiah shows us that evil was not built into creation by God as a sort of time-bomb; evil, though not created or desired by God, falls under his dominion and God will 'bring all things in heaven and on earth together under one head, even Christ' (Eph. 1:10).

When God had created the earth, space, plants, living creatures and the first human beings, he 'saw that it was very good' (Gn. 1:31). Evil came after that to spoil God's excellent creation. As people misused their God-given freedom and made bad choices, history turned into a catalogue of the struggles between good and evil. We no longer see God's creation as he intended it, 'very good'.

But Isaiah shows us that, despite and through history, God is unfolding his plan to salvage, to re-create, to save his creation. Suffering and evil are included in God's plan — evil is not another side to God's personality, not a necessary opposite force, irrevocably locked in battle with good, but evil is being transformed by God to become useful to him. In the words of the Apostle Paul 'we know that in all things God works for the good of those who love him' (Rom. 8:28).

God shows his superior wisdom and foresight by allowing that which he did not want. God wanted people who would choose to love him, freely, for his greatness and excellence alone. But creating people with freedom of choice meant that God had to allow for the awful possibility that they might reject him. He did not want it, but allowed for the possibility of it and took responsibility for the consequences.

Ever since Calvin explained how 'God has from the farthest limit of eternity decreed what he was going to do' (*Institutes*, 1.16.8) most Christians have believed the 'eternal and unchangeable counsel of God', namely that 'God from all eternity did freely and unchangeably ordain whatsoever comes to pass' (*Westminster Confession*, Ch.3). Also the 39 Articles of the Church of England refer to such an 'everlasting purpose' of God (Art.17).

For a long time after I first came across this concept of the 'counsel' of God, I found it very alien. It seemed so cold — such an eternally fixed plan seemed to destroy all freedom. It made history look like a video film, planned and edited by God; the only thing left is for it to be

122

shown. All seemed fixed in advance. Calvinistic thinking has often gone astray in this direction and I ignored the 'counsel' of God — it carried such a sense of deterministic finality about it. But now I have come to understand it in a new way which makes it useful for countering both monism and dualism.

In God's plan of salvation there are things which are not according to his desired will, things which do not mirror God's character of goodness and love, but things God still uses to achieve his good purpose. God's plan of salvation is being worked out through our history of chaos and suffering. God's 'counsel' is not for one moment loose from God himself; it is always under his control:

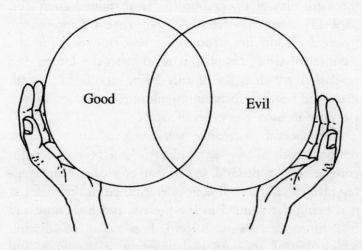

It is in the pierced hands of Christ that God carries all the good and evil that takes place in the world. Good and evil do not co-exist in God. Neither are they two opposite powers keeping each other in balance. Rather, in Christ, God holds both good and evil in his hand.

The prophecy of Isaiah 45 uses many images from nature — rain and germinating crops, light and darkness — and applies them to God's creative activity in history. The images tell us what is happening in our times — about the comings and goings of Saddam Hussein and 124 George Bush; Itzak Rabin and Yasser Arafat; Jerusalem and Babylon! God has called them all into being to fulfil his plans. It is God who acts and he alone, says Isaiah.

Isn't it amazing? No one and nothing else is working out history, but only the God of Israel, the God of the Bible — 'I am the LORD (YAHWEH, the covenant name of God), and there is no other god beside me. In my plans for the history of my creation I have decided to use good and evil, light and darkness, war and peace, so that soon the earth may be opened up to reveal righteousness' (Ps. 85:9–14). Many followers of Calvin have interpreted the 'counsel of God' in far too rigid a way. But Isaiah sees the 'counsel of God', his plan in relation to the future, as a revelation which is continually being unrolled . . . with space and freedom for meaningful human interaction. Yes, I believe in such a 'counsel of God'!

I accept this incredible third way as an alternative option which allows us to identify evil as evil, yet not completely outside God. God has an eternal and unchanging plan of salvation. It is not determined in the past, but it is being determined in the present and has a sure and final future *dénouement* in sight. It is a plan of salvation which uses all the hurt and suffering of the world and transforms them to become part of God's holy, good purpose. It is a plan of salvation which transforms the pain caused by sin into the birthpangs by which a pregnant creation is labouring to give birth to the kingdom of God (Rom. 8:22, Mk. 13:8). This birth takes time. It proceeds slowly. And in the meantime many mysteries remain. God willed what he did not want — even suffering — to end suffering; war to ban war; the crucifixion of Jesus to crucify death.

Those incomprehensible words of Isaiah become gospel words when he reminds the Jews of his day not to stop at the apparent suffering they will see, but to remember that they are God's creation. God invites them to ask him about their future so that they may gain confidence to entrust themselves, their children, and the work of their hands to him:

> I summon you by name . . . I will strengthen you , though you have not acknowledged me . . . I am the LORD, and there is no other . . . I form the light and create darkness . . . I create light and darkness, I bring prosperity and create disaster; I, the LORD, do all these things . . . Woe to him who quarrels with his Maker, to him who is but a potsherd among the potsherds on the ground. Does the clay say to the potter, 'What are you making?' Does your work say, 'He has no hands?' (Is. 45)

We, too, are invited to entrust ourselves, our loved ones and our work to the God who has us securely in his unfolding plan of salvation.

Future Things

In J.R. Tolkien's *The Lord of the Rings* the wicked Gollum helps Frodo to complete his mission. He grabs the ring from Frodo, falls into the fire and is destroyed along with his precious ring. It ends the stranglehold of evil, and Middle-Earth is saved. It also reminds me of what the Scriptures teach about suffering: 'Yes, even the land of darkness will know your glory' (Ps. 68:30–32; 87:4). I may safely entrust my future to God's mysterious, hidden acts of salvation. I can obey his call to pursue righteousness for in this world righteousness has received a new, deep meaning: God uses all things, even evil, to achieve his plan of salvation.

We know that this is so because of Calvary and Easter, when death was swallowed up in victory and despair became hope, a glimpse of the destination to which the 'third way' leads — the salvation of our God who is totally good and totally God. As we trust him, in and with our suffering, we become co-workers in his great plan of salvation for us and our children.

Summary

In times of great suffering, despair can so overcome us that we find it impossible to believe. It is very important to build our house of life on the rock before the storms come. That rock is the knowledge of God's 'counsel' of salvation, his sure desire and will to salvage and re-create his fallen creation. We need, however, both John and Isaiah to discover the deep and secret meaning of God's 'counsel' of salvation. As a third way, this 'counsel' is superior to both monism — the way which desecrates God's name (when he is seen as all-encompassing, incorporating good and evil within himself) — and dualism —

the way which demeans God's name (when he is seen as one of two equal but opposite forces locked in combat with no hope of victory). The God who wills what he does not want, and transforms even the evil he hates to make it meaningful and useful in his plan of salvation, he is the God to whom we may entrust our lives, also in our suffering. His sure 'counsel' is guaranteed in Jesus — for God will 'bring all things in heaven and on earth together under one head, even Christ' (Eph. 1:10).

Questions

1. Many people believe in evolution. Is an evolutionist a monist or a dualist?
2. Does it help to say to someone in distress, 'Do not ask why; just ask wherefore'?
3. Job recalls God's own words as testimony against God (Job 16). What do you think of his complaint in the light of this chapter?

Bible Readings

Genesis 1:31; Job 16; Psalm 68:30–32; 85:9–14; 87:4; Isaiah 45; Mark 13:8; Romans 8:22,28; Ephesians 1:10; 1John 1:5.

For Further Reading

Blocher, H. *Evil and the Cross* (Leicester: IVP, 1994)
Carson, D.A. *How long, O Lord?* (Leicester: IVP, 1991)
Kübler-Ross, E. *On Death and Dying* (New York: MacMillan, 1969)
Lewis, C.S. *The Problem of Pain* (Fount Paperbacks, 1993)
Schaeffer, E. *Affliction* (Carlisle: Solway, 1996)

7

Learning to Live with Suffering

In the previous chapter we have set suffering within the context of the teaching of the Bible and the 'eternal counsel' of God. We identified God's relationship to suffering and we touched on what our hope is when we suffer. In this chapter I will show how such a biblical framework can empower, change, encourage and motivate us in coping with our personal suffering and sorrow. How does a person handle the sudden, bitter, and dreadful news of the death of a loved one — a brother, a parent, a dear friend, a child . . .? How do I cope when my own body and mind is suddenly threatened and weakened by pain, regression or impending death? The Bible handles it — Job, for one, received such news.

Our contemporary Western culture gives us little preparation for our times of suffering. Everything around us is geared to ignore and marginalize death, sickness and suffering — to push them to the fringe as bothersome and inconvenient. They are problems we can take care of later. We are encouraged to think of the positive while we are healthy and fit. And indeed, thanks to the advances of medical science we can expect to go on being healthy, well into our old age. But the great emphasis on health and well-being has also made it more difficult to cope when suffering and sorrow come our way. We are not taught to expect it — on the contrary, we see it as abnormal, meaningless, a 'nasty shock'.

But, how can we give a meaningful role to suffering   129
and death in a culture saturated with a humanist view of life which has no place for God? This question surfaces regularly in debates concerning euthanasia. The person who sees suffering only as loss, a negative experience, wants to end it as quickly as possible. When improvement becomes unlikely, suffering loses meaning — surely it is meaningless then to suffer . . . Or can there be a meaningful role for suffering in our lives even in such circumstances?

Thorn in the Flesh

To answer these questions I turn to 2 Corinthians 12 where the Apostle Paul speaks about 'a thorn in my flesh' (vs. 7–10). This is his deeply personal testimony of how he learnt to go on living despite this 'thorn', and it is an object lesson to all of us.

What was Paul's 'thorn in the flesh'? Most commentators immediately link it to an illness, especially because of the words 'in the flesh'. But that is not necessarily true. A more accurate translation is 'thorn *for* the flesh', where the word 'flesh' refers to 'person'. Something had entered Paul's life, which irritated and upset his whole *person*. In these circumstances Paul borrowed the expression 'thorn in the flesh' from the Old Testament (Nu. 33:55). Here the LORD warned the people of Israel, 'But if you do not drive out the inhabitants of the land, those you allow to remain will become barbs in your eyes and *thorns in your sides*. They will give you trouble in the land where you

130 will live.' These 'thorns' produced the pain of unredeemed fragments in a liberated life — the irritating, painful pricking which would contine to remind the Israelites of the disobedience which caused their suffering.

So I tend to think of Paul's 'thorn' as a fragment of unredeemed life which again and again caused him great misery and trouble. In 2 Cor. 12:7 he even refers to this trouble as being caused by 'a messenger of Satan, to torment me'. What exactly his pain was, we're not told. But through it we get to know Paul as a vulnerable person. Some people connect this with Gal. 4:14,15 where Paul thanks the Galatians that they received him with such friendliness despite his serious eye infection. He says literally, 'Even though my illness was a trial to you, you did not treat me with contempt or scorn . . . I can testify that, if you could have done so, you would have torn out your eyes and given them to me.' But for all we know, that illness was healed by the time he wrote his second letter to the Corinthians. Perhaps by this time he suffered from migraine or depression. Some people have suggested that Paul suffered deep disappointment in a relationship, that he was deserted by someone he had cared for deeply. No one really knows the precise details. We can only guess about this penetrating fragment of unredeemed life. Maybe it's better that the nature of the complaint was left vague — maybe the vagueness was intentional so that we cannot be side-tracked, but rather take note of the way Paul dealt with it and so learn from him.

The really important question is how Paul handled his 'thorn'. The answer will also be of key importance to help us cope in our situations of personal suffering. We shall look at three successive stages in Paul's handling of his suffering, namely *aggressive protest*, *attentive faith*, and *quiet submission*. We need all three stages, and in the right order of succession, to find true biblical comfort. It is no good to look for short-cuts. They tend to leave us stranded, again to cry out, 'If only I could believe!'

Aggressive protest

The first thing which strikes me is Paul's *assertiveness*. He identifies his suffering as coming from Satan — 'a messenger of Satan' is tormenting him. He had no illusions about good and evil coming equally from God's hand. He experienced his suffering as a direct attack from the underworld — from 'a messenger of Satan'. When you are attacked so blatantly, you cannot ignore it, simply shrug your shoulders helplessly and endure it. Such a blatant enemy has to be arrested and opposed, aggressively, with all your strength, to be stopped in its tracks. Paul entered the battle, and he did it by praying to God in aggressive protest: 'Lord, take the messenger of Satan away; stop him; remove him.'

Prayer as protest. James also encourages his readers to tackle the fight in this way: 'Is any of you in trouble? He should pray . . . call the elders of the church to pray over him . . . And the prayer offered in faith will make the sick person well; the Lord will raise him up' (Jas. 5:13–15). The Greek word for 'make well', *soôzo,* can easily be translated as 'saved'. What James is saying, clearly, is to assure the believers that, in answer to the prayer of faith, saving power will go out from the risen Lord to combat the opponent. Sometimes it may result in physical healing but that is not the only way by which God shows his saving power.

The prayer of faith is, first, a *protest* against the illness — second, it is a request for healing. The first thing for Christians to do in conflict with illness or any form of unredeemed life, is not meekly to resign themselves to it but to resist it, aggressively, in faith. This sorrow does not come from God and in his name we may resist it. It is an attack from the evil one, God's enemy. We must not immediately allow ourselves to be knocked into depression or passivity; we must exert ourselves; fight with strength; use all our skill. When Jesus saw the sorrow of Martha and Mary after the death of their brother Lazarus, he became 'deeply moved in spirit and troubled' (Jn. 11:33). A very strong Greek word is used here and it is best translated as 'furious, raging'. Jesus was intensely angry about the wickedness which destroys human lives. It also justifies our being angry.

But against whom or what should we direct our anger? Against God? Paul focused on the real source of the evil — an angel of Satan, sent to torment him. Apparently the deep anger in Jesus was directed against the same arch-enemy of God. Why should he spoil God's handiwork?

Why should the inexpressible violence of death break up such an intimate brother-and-sister relationship? Jesus' anger expresses a strong inner resistance. Wickedness distorts life — it intentionally breaks life apart. So we can know for certain that we are on God's side when we resist suffering, when we voice our anger and deep disappointment, when we protest against illness and death.

Prayer as request. Prayer is our voice of protest, but the Scriptures encourages us also to *request* healing. It is not true that Christians have hope only for an afterlife. Someone once asked me whether socialists were right to blame Christians for having hope for a better world only in eternity, always saying, 'Be still, wait, be patient, all will be renewed . . .' The answer to such an accusation is: no. Christians should be first to resist suffering in this world. Christians, after all, know about another, God-intended world. This knowledge should make them oppose suffering aggressively, here and now. One way to fight suffering is to pray for healing. And God gives healing to show that he fights along with us, against decay and death.

But prayer for healing is, of course, not the only way to resist evil. The words we quoted from James 5 are preceded by an attack on the rich folk of his day: 'Your wealth has rotted, and moths have eaten your clothes. Your gold and silver are corroded.' James enters a fight against the social injustices of his day. And when it comes to illness he fights the same injustices and encourages us, too, to enter the fight. Often we are defeatist and unmotivated to resist.

The charismatic movements of our time have brought a widespread revival in our awareness of the biblical promises of healing and restoration to encourage our fight in prayer against the fallen brokenness of our existence. Indeed, the first calling of the church is to continue in prayer, full of faith — even when the patient seems to be without hope of restoration — proclaiming the resurrection power of Christ over death and decay. This is the strongest possible form of resistance against injustice, loneliness, physical and emotional pain.

Paul fought. He prayed to God to remove that 'messenger of Satan' from him. Perhaps he prayed like this: 'Lord God, it must be a small matter for you to break him, to defeat his destructive work and make it impossible for him to continue. You raised Christ from the dead and have already given Satan his death blow. Therefore I know, you can also remove this evil which troubles me.' The fighting spirit of Paul's aggressive prayer must be also our first reaction to suffering and wickedness, today.

Attentive faith

But though Paul faithfully followed the example of Jesus and bravely protested against his suffering, praying in the spirit of James 5, what he had asked for and hoped for with his whole heart, did *not* happen. The 'messenger of Satan' did not flee. Of course, we cannot deduce any rule or principle from the fact that Paul's prayer was unanswered (for instance, that God will always leave the evil to torment us, despite our prayers). That will make a mockery of James who promises us that in response to the prayer of faith a 'saving' will happen. So what should we make of Paul's experience?

Shortly after Paul's conversion he was miraculously healed from blindness. And on his later missionary travels he healed many blind and disabled people, raised a dead youth to life, and removed a poisonous snake from his own arm without any ill effects! Paul therefore had closely experienced healing in answer to prayer. It is precisely for that reason, he takes care in 2 Corinthians to explain that in this case no healing happened! But what *did* happen this time in response to his fervent prayer, repeated three times, made an everlasting impression on him.

It was as a messenger of God's good news, violently attacked by Satan and impeded by a painful fragment of unredeemed life, that Paul learned a new lesson from the Lord. He prayed once in protest; he prayed a second time, holding on to God's promise; he prayed a third time, trusting God completely. But his fervent requests were not granted. And then God taught him something very special — '*let my grace be enough!*' It was as if God said: 'At this moment, in the work I am giving you to do, you need only be a signpost to my grace. Let now my grace be sufficient for you. Because my power will be revealed most fully in your weakness.'

In coping with his suffering, Paul's uppermost commitment was to learn from it. When God's answer is not according to our expectations, we generally react quite differently — we either stubbornly persevere with our pleading prayers, or we give up all hope and give in to doubt and depression. On the one hand we are tempted by an obstinate attitude of 'God *must* do it — he promised healing' in which we stand over God and prescribe how he should act (a demanding tone often found in members of 'charismatic' and 'Pentecostal' churches). On the other hand we may be tempted to have a withdrawn, aloof attitude which excuses God's refusal by claiming that the ministry of healing is no longer intended for us, sometimes supported by quoting the writings of well-respected Christian leaders (an attitude of unbelief, disappointment and doubt often found in members of 'orthodox' or 'Reformed' churches).

God's megaphone. Paul had neither of these two attitudes. He didn't stubbornly persevere in claiming God's promise of complete healing, there and then. Neither did he give way to doubt and claim that the promise of healing had never been intended for him. No, Paul allows himself to be taught by God — he asks God to teach him. How will God use this undesirable and painful thorn in his flesh to achieve what could never have come about if God had granted his request? Did God have some other plan in mind? In *The Problem of Pain* (Ch. 6), C.S. Lewis remarks that 'God whispers to us in our joy, he speaks to us in our conscience, but he shouts to us in our suffering.' Our suffering can be the megaphone God uses to wake us up to a spiritual reality in our world.

To see our suffering in this light is an insight which is as much neglected today as our need to resist aggressively in faith. We sometimes forget that it is through suffering that God teaches us wisdom and perseverance. He may equally choose to take away our suffering — he is almighty; he can do it. But sometimes he chooses not to. Many people reject a God who does not directly remove or alleviate their suffering or that of their loved ones. But God can also use suffering to teach us — when we continue to look for *him,* in faith.

The same principle holds good for the nations of the world. When God's judgments go out over the earth, the nations learn justice (Is. 26:9). In response to monism which holds to a deity who combines good and evil in himself, we can reply, 'No, it is a messenger of Satan that brings my suffering.' We do not want to desecrate God's name by saying that evil comes from him. But we also do not want to demean God's name by pretending that suffering has nothing to do with God and takes place outside his authority. Paul teaches us to hold on to the fact of God's power over suffering by resisting in prayer, 'Three times I pleaded with the Lord to take it away from me. But he said to me, "My grace is sufficient for you, for my power is made perfect in weakness."' Such an answer from God tests our commitment to learning from him — sometimes it will lead us to ask, 'For what purpose is God allowing this to continue in my life?'

Transformation. The Lord entered Paul's life in an unexpected way when he did not remove the 'thorn'. Instead, he explained to Paul that this would be the means to keep him 'from becoming conceited because of these surpassingly great revelations', the means to keep Paul from becoming too self-sufficient. Satan sent the trouble intending to destroy Paul, to knock him down, but the Lord transformed the suffering and used its painful effect to make Paul even more useful to him, and more Christ-like — to preserve him and to lift him up. Now Paul could stand in front of people, not as a monument of strength and deliverance, one to be admired, but instead, as an ordinary, troubled and weak person; but one who was being supported in an amazing way by an awesome God!

138

How is it possible to radiate peace when one is seriously ill? How is it possible for someone who has suffered abuse and emotional neglect to resist bravely? Such strength comes from beyond the person concerned. To see it in action often speaks more powerfully than a hundred model sermons delivered by the most skilful preachers — it is a real-life, 3-D demonstration of God's power at work in human vulnerability and weakness.

It reminds me of a Dutch minister. A tragic bus accident in Rev Woelderink's parish killed a number of children, including three of his own. People still remember how, on the first Sunday after their bereavement, in the midst of the heartache and pain, he said, 'for one moment I was filled with such joy in the Lord, that, had he asked me to part with all my children for his sake, I would gladly have given them to him.' The testimonies of Corrie ten Boom and Joni Eareckson, to mention only two, are similar.

Paul was not just *used* by God — he experienced, deeply, that the wretched thorn in the flesh drew him closer to God. As he became more and more dependent on the power of Christ he became more and more familiar with the safety within God's merciful goodness. Paul learnt from what he suffered that he could depend on God, and he learnt humility. Like Job he learnt patience, and he learnt to honour God's majesty. All God's people have to learn these things — even Jesus 'learnt obedience from what he suffered, and, once made perfect, he became the source of eternal salvation for all who obey him' (Heb. 5:7–10).

However, in facing suffering this should never be our first response. Our first response, always, must be righteous anger, resistance, and earnest prayer for restoration and healing. The person who immediately responds, sighing 'his grace is sufficient for you', has no understanding, no mercy, and little sympathy. The transformation of our suffering happens only inside that intimate relationship with God himself. No one else can make it happen for you — no words can bring it about. It is an understanding and knowledge which grows out of the secret, personal and intimate whisperings of God's Spirit into your heart.

After Job suffered a multitude of uncanny disasters, his friends came to encourage him. They kept silent for seven days and seven nights as they sat with him. During that time they shared his struggle. If only they had continued to do that! It was after that first week that they started going wrong — they became impatient and wanted Job to get to a quick answer. But they said foolish things about God, things that were not true or right — while Job, even in his bitter complaints, never sinned against God. God teaches us through our sufferings; he reveals his wisdom to us. But we are not to blame God as if he brought our suffering about, caused it and desired it to happen, not even in order to teach or punish us. God uses suffering — he transforms the pain to show his mercy and goodness — but he does it individually, and he does it in his own time.

139

There are no rules, no 'quick-fixes', no time-schedules in godly grieving, sorrowing, suffering.

Quiet submission

140 Finally, the third stage: determined resignation, despair, denial . . . what is the final result in our lives of continuing suffering? For Paul it was quiet submission as he concluded: 'Therefore I will boast all the more gladly about my weaknesses, so that Christ's power may rest on me. That is why, for Christ's sake, I delight in weaknesses, in insults, in hardships, in persecutions, in difficulties. For when I am weak, then I am strong' (2 Cor. 12:9).

Some people might dismiss this as an example of 'typical Pauline spiritual masochism'. Paul really suffered because of the thorn in his flesh. But he did not thank God for the pain itself. On the contrary, he gave thanks for what God was achieving in him — using suffering to make him teachable and to produce a harvest in his life. The pain did not purify Paul; God did. Especially in Paul's words, 'When I am weak, then I am strong', I sense a hint of the quiet submission which characterizes this third stage.

On the one hand weak, defenceless, injured; on the other hand strong, powerful, and useful to God. Yes, such a wonderful transformation is possible only in the kingdom of God. 'When I am weak, then I am strong', was not just a typical 'stiff upper lip' way for a high-flyer like Paul to respond; he had been painfully honest in describing his real suffering and humiliation. His confident submission was the result of seeing a supernatural harvest in his life which far outweighed the cost of his suffering.

This reminds me of Heb. 12:11: 'No discipline seems pleasant at the time, but painful. Later on, however, it produces a harvest of righteousness and peace.'

The harvest is God's will being done, powerfully, in our weakness. I myself have seen such a harvest and such peace in believers who have passed through a dark struggle of deep suffering, people who could only rest in the grace given them in Christ. For in the cross of Christ God gave us everything: he went ahead and passed through death for us; he suffered all we could possibly suffer. But the cross is empty. Christ was raised and in his resurrection revealed life.

Contented submission is not passive surrender; it is active perseverance, based on the sure knowledge that our suffering is achieving a great harvest. And the strength to persevere comes from Christ's fullness of life, freely available, now and forever — we can rely on it in faith.

Seeing the Image Appear

Through fighting bravely, resisting aggressively, and learning from God's answers to our prayers, we finally become useful to God. It is the ultimate aim of a Christian to become a living signpost to Christ, 'the wounded Healer'. The church of Christ is not the source of light. Instead, it is a beam of light reflected from the Son of Righteousness to shine on life in the dark corners of this world. In order to reflect his light we need to become mirrors of God's image. But that is possible only when our old desires die. We need to be changed so that we no longer find meaning for our lives in independence, strength, health, wealth and friends.

142 We need to become related to God in a new way. And it happens as we allow him to use our sufferings to purify us, in the same way as a silversmith purifies silver (Mal. 3:3). The craftsman extracts the silver by smelting a mixture of ores at high temperatures. When the alloy is further melted a layer of lead oxide and other impurities forms on the surface of the crucible like a dark shadow. This dross is skimmed away or run off to leave the purified silver behind. Only when the silversmith can see the reflection of his own face in the crucible (as in a mirror) does he know that his job is done. This is a lovely image of how God changes us. He waits till he can see the refelection of his own face, radiating goodness and love, mirrored in our faces — only then is his work done. He is committed to use whatever it takes, even the suffering and pain Satan produces to destroy us, in order to purify us till his image appears, perfectly reflected.

Summary

Many problems arise when we deal with sorrow and suffering. Some people see protest as the only devout reaction while others see it as a sign of unbelief. Resignation to our suffering may sound very pious, but it is sometimes the protest of the faithless. With the Lord Jesus himself and Paul and James as our guides we have examined how to handle our suffering. There are three successive stages in the process of coping with suffering:

struggling and resisting in *aggressive protest*, especially in prayer; w*aiting patiently* and *learning* from God's answers to our prayers; and *submitting quietly*, which includes persevering and identifying how God is transforming us into his image — making us more useful to him in our vulnerability.

All three stages are essential, in the right order of succession, if we are to become useful to God — shortcuts only undermine our faith and leave us, again, to cry out, 'If only I could believe!'

Questions

1. There are many forms of suffering . Is it possible that we can learn to deal with them all, in all circumstances, at all times?
2. Is all suffering purifying?
3. In what way is the suffering of Jesus, and the way he dealt with it, unique?

Bible Readings

Numbers 33:55; Isaiah 26:9; Malachi 3:3; John 11:33; 2 Corinthians 12:7–10; Galatians 4: 14,15; James 1; 5:13–15; Hebrews 5:7–10; 12:11.

For Further Reading

Lewis, C.S. *Till we have Faces* (Glasgow: Collins, 1983)
—— *A Grief Observed* (Faber, 1966)

Johnson, D., Van Vonderen, J. *The Subtle Power of Spiritual Abuse*, Part III (Minnesota: Bethany House Publishers, 1991)

Nouwen, H. *The Ultimate Gift — a meditation on dying and caring* (Doubleday)

Silvester, H. *Arguing with God* (Leicester: IVP)

Thielicke, H. *Waiting Father* (Cambridge: Clarke, 1960)

144

8

Uniqueness, Identity and Faith

'*So you feel you have many personalities?*' the psychiatrist
said cautiously to Wim.

'Yes, we do,' Wim replied cheerfully.

'*And do the voices of these other personalities speak to you?*'

'We talk to each other sometimes.'

'*Do some of your selves frighten you?*'

'*Of course not*', said Wim.

'*Which of your selves do you like best?*'.

'*Each of us likes himself the best.*'

'*But which do* **you** *like best?*' insisted the psychiatrist.

'*Me.*'

'*Who is "me"?*'

'*Me-here-now*', said Wim.

'*What's "me-here-now" like?*'

'He's like "him-there-then" only a few seconds ago. Now the
one I like best is the new 'me-here-now.''''

'*I see*', said the psychiatrist, frowning and scribbling rapidly.
'*Don't you feel any continuity between your consecutive
selves?*'

'Oh sure,' said Wim. 'We all think our predecessors are fools.'

'*What do you want to do with your life?*'

'*Whose life?*'

'*The lives of yourselves.*'

'Oh, we all have different plans,' said Wim.
'Well, what determines which one of you acts at any given moment?'
Wim smiled. 'Ignorance and Chance,' he replied.
(From *Adventures of Wim* by Luke Rhinehart, p.216)

146

Many great writers have explored the idea of a diversity of personalities existing within each individual person and struggling for control at any given moment. So Goethe's (1749-1832) Faust says: 'Two souls are living in my breast.' And the main character in *Der Steppenwolf* by Hermann Hesse (1877–1962) responds to these words by exclaiming that 'with me there are many conflicting personalities in my breast — sometimes I am a mauling lion, then again a meek lamb; now I recognize a maniac in myself, then again a saint.' Psychotherapists have studied and applied this idea in the treatment of their patients — by encouraging them to identify their different selves and to act them out in roleplay. In the transactional analysis of Thomas A. Harris (*I'm OK — you're OK*), for instance, the patient learns to recognize first the 'parent' within themself, next the 'child', then the 'adult'.

In the quoted extract from *Adventures of Wim*, in answer to 'Who is "me"?', Wim replies, 'me-here-now'. But even as he says it, that self has passed. So, are we all like this? Or is there a single, unique, most intimate self at the core of our personal being? How should we define our 'self' and which things may prevent us from finding our personal uniqueness? This is what this final chapter is all about.

Identity, Inner Self, Uniqueness

The Norwegian dramatist Ibsen (1828–1906) did not see 'inner self' as a concrete core, central to our personality. Rather, he preferred to compare the inner self with an onion — as you peel away the layers, what do you find? Not a solid core, but a hole in the air, nothing! (*Peer Gynt*, 1867) The person who searches inside themselves for such a 'core', going deeper and deeper, at best finds a chain of DNA molecules. But DNA still cannot explain all the complex facets of individual personality.

The psychoanalyst Eric Ericson (1902–1994) described identity — 'who you really are' — as that which runs like a red thread through all the stages of a person's individual development and through all the 'layers' of their personality. Therefore, looking at a photograph of your mother, you can say, 'That is typical of her — her expression, her manner.' Maybe it is the way a person scratches their head, or wrinkles their nose when they laugh, the rhythm of their footsteps or the way they prepare to clear their throat . . . When we try to think why a particular expression or gesture is so typical of someone, we realize that personality is a complex matter; many facets contribute to a person's uniqueness.

In order to explain the workings of personality, the founder of psychoanalysis, Sigmund Freud (1856–1939), explained the intricate workings of the inner self by referring to an *ich*, an *über-ich*, and an *es*. Many psychologists and counsellors have used a three-fold division to describe the workings of the inner self. Personality is often discussed in relation to a *factual I*, an *actual I* and a *normative*

I. The 'factual I' is my personality as seen through the eyes of other people who observe my behaviour. The 'actual I' is the part of my personality which is not so easily observed from outside — only the person who looks very carefully will correctly identify those characteristic long-ings and moods which define my 'actual I' and determine my behaviour. The 'normative I' is the person I am striving to become, according to my norms and values — but, by definition, this 'normative I' remains an ideal self, a self I never completely achieve.

148

In considering these different approaches, I agree with Hermann Hessse that there seem to be many subdivisions within the personality of a person. Older books often illustrated it with an 'enneagram' which describes human personality in relation to nine defined animal character types — the tiger, the owl, the cat, the buffalo, the butterfly, the pigeon, the deer, the black stallion and the ant. There is a sound basis for Luke Rhinehart's descrip-tion of the dialogue with Wim at the beginning of this chapter — many people experience themselves as having such varied personalities, identities with no 'common denominator', no unifying inter-connection. If this is true and there is no single, unique core to personal being, are we all then destined to continue in hopelessly *fragmented* lives?

Post-modernism

The tendency to doubt the uniqueness of personal being is part of what we call 'post-modernism'. Luke Rhinehart is a post-modern writer and it is significant to note how the quoted dialogue ends — for if no single core-identity exists to determine our behaviour, then ignorance and chance are left to determine our actions at any given time. Such reasoning opens up an excellent way of escape, for no one can lead a responsible life under the domination of such ever-changing personalities!

The writings of Michel Foucault (1926–1988) continue to be very popular and influential. His pluralistic description of personality suits our pluralistic Western culture very well. According to him, different personalities emerge within a person in response to the stimuli of the many and varied circumstances of life. There is no single 'ideal' personal self. On the contrary, to talk of a single kind of personal existence as 'ideal', something to strive for as individuals is exactly *the* danger we need to avoid. We need to resist group pressure, middle-class values, 'streamlining'. According to Foucault it is the duty of each person to deny that 'ideal' self, promoted by social and religious pressure. Be careful, he warns, for the next step is into a straitjacket!

I can understand Foucault's protest. This, too, is part of post-modern thinking. But in his protest against becoming bourgeois and giving in to group pressure, he assumed the existence of an inner core, an inner self behind a person's multiplicity of personalities, a free 'core' which is in control of their decision making. Philosophers call such a core the 'free subject' — that which decides and chooses. How else is it possible for a person to reject a group identity? But as soon as you presuppose some free core deep inside the self, the same set of questions surfaces again. For, is such a core a person's factual I, actual I or normative I? Or is it a mystical depth-core which precedes all of their other selves?

New Ageism

150 Many people who are more mystically inclined experience an inner self, hidden behind their multiple personalities. I will call it the 'Self'. *Eastern religious thinking,* which underlies much New Age thinking, sees the soul of a person as coinciding with the soul of God (Atman and Brahman). The purpose of achieving oneness with my Self is so that my soul may be reconnected with God's soul, and so that God may have the possibility of expressing himself through me. Where this is achieved the human personality becomes ever more like a pond which mirrors the whole of reality — the deer drinking its water, the sun, moon, stars, clouds, butterflies and trees. The God of the East *is* all. Eastern mysticism assumes a deep 'god' core within each person — the uniqueness of humankind *is* the uniqueness of God. But if God's personal being coincides with human personal being, what space is there left for uniqueness in personhood?

Western mysticism is very similar to the Eastern mysticism in New Age thinking. It teaches that people, by turning back into themselves, continue to be liberated from all their compulsive, struggling selves. Those selves were never essentially part of *them*, but have come about as a result of pressure from other people and situations. Pragmatically this mysticism 'works' well in our stressed and time-precious prosperity culture — for just 15 minutes of transcendental meditation is sure to relieve you of the pressing burdens of affluence!

There is a danger in this emphasis on finding your inner Self by turning inwards and emptying your consciousness of all outside memories and impressions. As with peeling an onion, such a person might find that, having stripped off layer upon layer of unique, inter-human experience, they are left, not with a divine core, but with profound emptiness, a feeling of total meaninglessness, alienation. What was hailed as the pinnacle of self-discovery, then feels more like the pinnacle of self-estrangement.

This is one way to achieve inner unity. Is there another way, an alternative way to that of post-modernism and New Ageism, by which to find my unique, individual, inner self and achieve inner unity?

The Bible

This question of the inner self confronts many people, when they consider becoming Christians. A question which often makes it impossible for them to commit themselves to God, is whether becoming a believer means losing their unique identity?

Young people and teenagers especially, in the exciting stage of discovering who they really are, become afraid when they hear a call to deny themselves, to take up their cross and to follow Jesus. Does this mean that they have to change their personality in order to become a follower of Christ? Is this call to self-denial also a call to self-rejection? Most people intuitively feel that this is bad news. And I agree. So, what *does* the Bible say about personality, identity and uniqueness?

Gn 1:27 says that 'God created man *in his own image*, in the image of God he created him; male and female he created them.' The animals and the plants were created after their own kind, but God created the first people after his own image — God brought them into being as separate from his self, but as selves similar to him.

In the Bible God reveals himself as both *personal* and *infinite*. God is on the one hand merciful (personal) and on the other hand he is almighty (infinite). It is very important to understand both these sides of God — the personal and the infinite — and how they relate to God's works in creation.

Personhood implies the ability to love, choose, create, communicate, respond. In that respect God created human beings to be his friends and partners, people to enjoy his creation and take part in developing it, people to relate to God and act creatively in response to his love with deeds of loving worship. As far as personality is concerned, God and his human creatures are alike, and together they differ from the rest of creation; as far as personality is concerned, humankind is unique in creation. This is a distinction of great importance, one not recognized by those evolutionists who see human beings only in their physical shape as developed from the animals, and ignore their personality in which they image God.

However, God is also *infinite*. In this aspect of his personality God differs from all of his creation, both humankind and nature. As people we are mortal like the flowers, and the insects, and the animals — St Francis was right when he spoke about 'Sister Moon' and 'Brother Wolf'. In our finiteness we are as far removed from God as all his other creatures; as finite creatures we are one with nature — the evolutionists are right — we are only another species. This resemblance explains, for instance, the intuition by which the early authors of the enneagram could identify human personality with animal types.

153

It is both the mystery and the dilemma of humankind that in their personal being they are like God — different from all the rest of creation — but that in their finiteness they are like the rest of creation — different from God. The following diagram illustrates it:

Personal:	Infinite:
God	God
Human beings	
	Human beings
Animals	Animals
Plants	Plants
Machines	Machines

What is Unique, Personal Identity?

We have seen that personal identity is of vital importance to many people. The Bible gives us a basis for believing in personal uniqueness: God created each human being personally in his image. That image has been distorted, but Christ came to redeem and recover it. The image of God as a unique, personal being is very specific to Judaism, Christianity and, with slight variations, to Islam. It differentiates these religions from Eastern religions which, although they also speak about God as a 'person', use it as a figure of speech to indicate the personification of a God who is, by nature, impersonal. Eastern religions worship an eternal God who is present *in* all things. There is no basis on which to distinguish between God and his creatures. Personal identity, therefore, does not exist, because the divine is locked up in all of creation.

So, what is the uniqueness that the Bible speaks about? To answer this question, first try to identify when it is that you feel most completely, uniquely your*self*? Surely it is in face to face, intimate relationship with another person who knows you, accepts you unconditionally and loves you, that you feel most completely and uniquely yourself.

Therefore I like to think of the most personal, inner self of each person as a unique *secret*, a secret which will develop and unfold itself only *within a love relationship*. It is very important not to see the uniqueness of a person as a substance deep inside their body or soul. Those who look for such uniqueness invariably discover that they are more like the onion than the tulip — having peeled all the leaves off a tulip you come to the core where the seed is hidden. But having done the same with an onion you are left with a handful of skins . . . there is no inner core. This is a startling and shocking discovery for many people. Uniqueness is not a deep-down, core characteristic — the theologian Helmut Thielicke (1908–86) called it an 'outeristic' (my translation), a redemption. It is not some *thing* you carry inside yourself; rather, it is what you find emerging *out* of yourself when you live in a love relation-ship. Your personal uniqueness and identity unfolds itself through the loving relationships within which God has placed you. If you fail in these relationships your unique-ness is going to suffer; you might even lose it. But if your relationships are healthy and loving, then you grow more and more into your personal uniqueness.

This also explains why bereavement is such an intense assault on our sense of identity and uniqueness. Identity is not a stagnant, inner characteristic. Identity grows and develops into fullness within a love relationship. To use Jesus' apt illustration, it is like a grape which ripens as long as it stays connected to the vine (Jn. 15:4).

Ultimately it is in relationship with *God* that we are most perfectly loved; there we are most perfectly identi-fied. In the parable of the prodigal son, the lost son returns to his father and says, 'I am no longer worthy to be called your son' (Lk. 15:21). In other words, his sonship was no longer a deep-down, assumed fact on which he could base his uniqueness and identity. He had spoiled things too badly; he had destroyed the relationship. So the son, rightly, says, 'I am no longer worthy to be called your son.' But his father answers, 'Quick! Bring the best robe . . . Put a ring on his finger . . . this son of mine . . . was lost and is found' (15:24). By re-affirming their relationship, the father restored the son's unique sense of identity — as a gift of mercy.

It is true that we are not worthy to be called 'children of God'. *We are all lost children in Adam.* When, in Adam, we broke off our relationship with God, we became rebels. Is there any trace left of our previous identity? When John Calvin (1509–1564) talks about our fallen state, he describes human nature as a 'residue' and 'misshapen ruins' (*Institutes*, II.II.12), fragments of the image of God, little 'sparks' left behind. It reminds me of an old-fashioned gramophone record. Imagine that I had found a broken fragment of a record and that, when I moved the needle of a record player over the fragment, I could recognize the opening chords of the fifth symphony of Beethoven on it! It could only happen if I knew the music very well. Similarly, we all have experienced many damaging relationships — these have shattered our personal sense of identity. The Bible is clear about this. But the Bible is not without hope, for in each person there are fragments left of the image of God. And sometimes in talking to someone you get a glimpse of their God-intended self — you see Christ in them (Eph. 4:15).

Fragments

The Fall has seriously impacted our unique sense of personal identity. The record is broken. But it is not completely useless. Since the Fall fragments of the image of God have been left behind, in all people — glimpses of how God had intended us to be, uniquely, in our actions, morality, choices. Fortunately God is the composer and the conductor: he knows the music intimately. He can reconstruct the whole symphony from a few distorted bars. God's salvation aims to repair the uniqueness of our personalities. We see this clearly in the actions of Jesus during his life on earth. He did not concentrate on stage-directed mass-meetings; he had deeply *personal* relation-ships with *individual* persons. In his conversation with the Samaritan woman he used an everyday image, water, to make her face up to her sinful lifestyle; in conversation with the Pharisee Nicodemus Jesus pushed him to the limit of his understanding with a 'shocking' use of the image of birth; Jesus put the self-conscious Zaccheus in the limelight to encourage him to actively change his way of life. Each interaction aimed to respond, uniquely, to the specific brokenness in the person. In John's gospel (ch. 10) Jesus calls himself 'the good shepherd . . . I know my sheep and my sheep know me.'

The Bible does not use the word 'identity'. But we do find again and again in the Bible that God *names* people and that new names signify a new and special relationship with him. When Jesus entered a relationship with Peter, he changed his name. It also happened to Paul, and much earl-ier, to Abraham, Sarah, Jacob. God, who recognizes what he hears when he puts his needle on the fragment, can per-fectly restore the music. Then the *name* begets the *person*!

Sometimes the work of the Holy Spirit sounds suspi-ciously as if it is to make us 'lose' our minds, to set us free from our factual selves. But the Bible describes 'being filled' by the Holy Spirit as a process in which I do not step out of myself, into ecstasy, but in which I come more and more into my true and unique self. The Holy Spirit leads each person *into* their God-given personal uniqueness.

In 1 Corinthians 12–14, Paul further emphasizes that the Spirit is given for the well-being of all the believers *together* and that each person has a unique contribution — each member of the body is indispensable to the whole (cf. Eph. 4:14–16). The Holy Spirit unfolds that individual uniqueness and he does it by giving us gifts! The fruit of the Spirit is the same for each member, but the gifts of the Spirit are uniquely tailored to express each person's individual uniqueness. That individual uniqueness is not a new identity given to me; it is the repaired version of the impaired person I was before I believed.

What Undermines Growth into Uniqueness?

The Bible gives us an understanding of the nature of our personal uniqueness (an image of God) — and a description of how to identify and develop our personal uniqueness (in loving relationships with God and other people). But we are far from what we should be. We are often confused about our identities.

And when we try to hide or mask our confusion, it shows itself in a multitude of symptoms. We can each identify with some of the following typical feelings:

• an exaggerated fear of making mistakes which traps us in perfectionism — my clothes must fit perfectly, no speck of dust is to be seen.

• an embarrassing shyness which makes me blush at unpredictable moments — I feel uncomfortable and I am not in control.

- great difficulty in sharing my personal thoughts and emotions with other people so that they often say, 'It is difficult to make real contact with her'.
- difficulty to find a balance in intimacy — we either stay too aloof or try too hard to be pleasing and fit in.

The question in the background is always the same: 'Who am I?'

159

'Sometimes I have the frightening feeling that my identity has collapsed, that deep down no one is there,' a girl admits to Christopher Lasch in *The Culture of Narcissism*. When this happens you feel as if all that you have achieved is falling apart and that you can no longer enjoy anything. At this point it is time to take action.

What are the obstacles we need to overcome in order to progress towards a secure awareness of our uniqueness and identity? From the preceding chapters of this book you might guess some: perfectionism, guilt (or is it shame?), anxiety, bereavement . . .

Is it possible that there is an underlying obstacle which causes all these varied symptoms? If I read Genesis 1–3, I see how the loss of a relationship with God led directly to shame, fear, and loss of intimacy. Furthermore, human-kind lost their dominion, the power to be master and ruler over nature (Gn 4:7). So much seems to hinge on that personal relationship with the unique, eternal God who made us and who, in love, wants us to be here.

What Encourages Growth into Uniqueness?

Did Zaccheus, the little tax-collector with the low self-esteem, secretly long for Jesus to help him in his miserable loneliness when he hid up the sycamore tree? Jesus noticed him and said, 'I am coming to tea at your house tonight' (Lk. 19:5)! There is help for all of us, and practical guidelines for becoming more of the person God intended us to be:

160

a) 'I am more'

God who made me, accepts me in Christ. Who then am I not to accept myself? Self-acceptance does not mean that I like all I do or say. Just as no parent likes all that their children do or say, yet still accepts them through thick and thin, despite their actions, so I should not reject myself in my failure, fear, or shame. Instead, I can start by believing that I am wanted as a person, for God intended me to be. Therefore I can grow into that unique person whom God already sees in me, completed. It reminds me of the sculptor who was chipping away at a piece of granite. When a passer-by stopped and asked him what on earth he was doing, he quietly answered, 'I'm releasing the angel locked up in here.'

Self-acceptance means accepting that I am *more* than the sum total of my failings and faults. The Apostle Paul said, 'if I do what I do not want to do . . . it is no longer I who do it, but it is sin living in me' (Rom. 7:16,17). He was not just making an excuse for his actions; immediately before this Paul took full responsibility for his sin (vs. 9).

Self-acceptance is the art of accepting as a gift the good things you do, and *enjoying* it. It is not something to be proud of — for, what do you have that has not been given to you? But it is something to acknowledge with thanks and to use with confidence. We often allow ourselves to be limited in our uniqueness. 'You cannot do that,' said his grandfather. And it took the grandson a whole lifetime to find out that he was capable of that which his grandfather doubted. Some limits are real — without a bicycle you cannot become an Olympic cyclist; a serious heart-defect disqualifies you from becoming an astronaut. But few limits are absolute — there are world-class musicians who are tone-deaf, and one-handed pianists! Many of our imagined limits have come to us through frivolous or undiscerning remarks by people who knew us little.

b) Don't measure yourself against others

When you measure yourself against others, you make yourself dependent on their judgment. This is what the Pharisees did. Jesus said to them, 'How can you believe if you accept praise from one another, yet make no effort to obtain the praise that comes from the only God?' (Jn. 5:44). It leads to stagnation. Today we are very sensitive to what other people might think. Words written by Pascal in the seventeenth century are as applicable today (*Pensées*, no. 806):

> *We are not satisfied with the life we have in ourselves and in our own being. We want to lead an imaginary life in the eyes of others, and so we try to make an impression. We strive constantly to embellish and preserve our imaginary being, and neglect the real one. And if we are calm, or generous, or loyal, we are anxious to have it known so that we can attach these virtues to our other existence; we prefer to detach them from our real self so as to unite them with the other. We would cheerfully be cowards if it would aquire us a reputation for bravery. How clear a sign of the nullity of our own*

being that we are not satisfied with one without the other and often exchange one for the other! For anyone who would not die to save his honour would be infamous.

Pascal says that we would gladly become cowards if it would give others the impression that we were brave!

162

Jesus warns us against such dependence on the opinions of other people — his gospel is therefore seriously anti-middle-class. Christians are not persons who strive to blend in with the crowd. Rather, the better we know God and ourselves, the more distinct we become in our uniqueness. Birdsong is much more splendid in the forest, sung to the glory of God, than at a fair, sung to please its trainer. Such inner freedom demands courage — sometimes to break away from restraining situations, sometimes to ignore the voices urging us to conform. Always remember that you live, ultimately, before the eyes of God, to please him, independently of what other people might think. Sometimes (*not* always) it might even mean that you say, 'What they think, does not concern me in the least.'

c) Learn from your mistakes and build on what you have achieved

Christians are encouraged, daily, to 'take off the old and to put on the new' (Col. 3:9,12). Paul uses the image of changing clothes to illustrate that this should be an almost automatic part of our lives. 'The old' is my self with its imperfections; 'the new' is my self as God sees me through Christ; 'taking off' implies that I am no longer burdened by it. The person who experiences each mistake as a confirmation of their unworthiness, finds it hard to take off the old. They would rather put on the new over the old. But no one can live and wear a hundred coats! Again and again the old will stick out, when a mistake or failure makes them vulnerable to the opinions of other people. But 'taking off' the old means that you have recognized it as a bad fit, an unflattering colour or style. And in the process you have learnt what suits you best.

To become *mature* is to become aware of, and to enjoy, who you are. It is achieved by building on your victories. It reminds me of an American burger, which you make by adding alternate layers of bread and filling until a mouthwatering feast has been created. That is how you should celebrate the victories in your personal growth into uniqueness and maturity!

d) Seven guidelines

Sometimes a crisis of circumstances or weak or sinful mismanagement might plunge a person back into the sinking feeling that they are losing their identity. There is always a way back to wholeness. The following are guidelines for getting back on track:

a) Follow the example of Daniel. Daniel and his friends kept to the rules of God's law in the Babylonian court despite pressure and temptation to abandon it (Dn. 1). The Lord rewarded their obedience and they outperformed the top-trained Babylonian youths who had followed regimes of special diets and exercises! God's commands are good for people — you always gain from obeying them.

b) Choose good role models. Self-image plays an important part in shaping your personality — and determining your norms and values. What shapes your ideal image? Heroes from Hollywood or saints of God? You lose out when you stop reading about the lives of men and women of God — people like Hudson Taylor, Corrie ten Boom, Joni Eareckson, Jackie Pullinger, Dietrich Bonhoeffer, Henri Nouwen, Terry Waite . . .

c) Discipline your time. A mature person is someone who knows how to spend their time wisely. Ask any high-flyer! The wise way of using your time includes space for God, to allow him to set the priorities for your day. Some people fear that a regulated existence will become a burden and create undue pressure. But a disorganized lifestyle brings the same pressure, not least the pressure of constant thoughts of regret — not enough time, again, for my children . . . parents. . . partner . . . friends . . .

d) Choose good friends. Good friends dare to tell you the truth. There is no perfect church, but woe to the congregation where people try only to please each other and dare not speak the truth for fear of division and disunity. It is always in relationship with those who love you that you find your identity. John called love for one another the 'mark' of a Christian (1 Jn. 5:1). Proverbs says that 'iron sharpens iron' (Pr. 27:17) — in an honest relationship the sparks may fly, but the blade is sharpened.

e) Be filled with the Holy Spirit. Does this sound trite and pious? I mean it quite practically, like Paul in Eph. 5:18 when he contrasts being filled with the Spirit to being filled with strong alcoholic drink. It is quite amazing that if a person walks by the Spirit and draws daily strength from their connection to God, they do not float off into oblivion, but walk solidly on the earth, able to distinguish soberly between truth and falsehood. Such a walk depends on regular times with God alone.

f) Do not forget that there is a great opponent. Sometimes trouble comes our way and we cannot understand what caused it. Satan uses our weaknesses — it is good to be on guard against him at all times, for in one moment of weakness he can destroy what has been achieved over many years. We do not fight against flesh and blood, says the Apostle Paul (Eph. 6:12), but against powers of wickedness in the heavenly realms.

g) Finally, keep hold of the 'royal sceptre'. In the series of adventure stories for children by John White, *The Anthropos Archives*, the most important advice to the adventurers is always to 'keep hold of the sceptre'. For us it means to keep hold of our uniqueness in Christ — who we are, in him — and not to get overwhelmed by our circumstances and our God-given responsibilities. Rather, we may meditate on the image of Jesus standing in the sailing boat and, in God's name, quieting down the raging stormwaves (Lk. 8:24).

The White Stone

To me there is a final promise which completes what the Bible teaches about personal identity, unity, and uniqueness. It is locked up in a verse in Revelation which we easily overlook, a verse filled with mysteriousness. Rev. 2:17 says, 'To him who overcomes . . . I will also give . . . a white stone with a new name written on it, known only to him who receives it' (Rev. 2:17).

This image comes from the Old Testament and is greatly expanded here in Revelation. For when the high-priest of the old covenant served in the Tabernacle and later in the Temple, he 'carried' the twelve 'children' of Israel on his heart, with a stone to represent each tribe (Ex. 39:8–18). And on that day when our high priest of the new covenant, Jesus, presents each individual person who has overcome the evil one in his name to his Father, they will be identified by a new name, engraved on a white stone, a secret name known only to God himself and the person who receives it. The image speaks powerfully of our unique identity, for in the Bible a person's *name* is usually a meaningful expression of their personality. 'Eve', 'Jacob', 'Naomi', 'Peter', to mention only a few, were given prophetic names at crucial times in their lives. The *colour* of the stone is also significant. It speaks of being specially chosen. It speaks also of cleansing, purification, completion — all qualities which are symbolized in the Bible by the colour white. Finally the image indicates intimacy — a *secret* name — a most intimate moment, *the* fulfilment of all our deepest longings for intimacy when we will be known, at last, fully and perfectly.

As a beam of light breaks into a rainbow of colours when it passes through a prism, each person who comes to God in the name of Jesus receives a dazzling revelation of their God-given uniqueness when God names them — 'just between me and you, this is who I made you to be.' There is no other philosophy, world-view, god, or psychological insight that can promise us such self-knowledge and significance — it is the unique promise of the Bible.

If only . . . ? You, too, *could* . . . ! If you have been honest about your disappointment in God, if you have addressed your hidden fears, if you are learning step by step to grow in trust, if you have confessed your guilt and examined your shame, if you have come to understand where you are on your journey of life, if you have faced your despair and have overcome your suffering, you too may look forward, in hope, to that certain day in the future when you will see the LORD, and know yourself as you are known by your Maker, Father and Healer.

Summary

In this chapter the biblical basis for believing in the uniqueness of personal being is compared with the teachings of post-modernism and New Ageism. Uniqueness of personality is explained in terms of being created in the image of God, made for a relationship with him and with

168 other people. The question is examined whether coming to faith means that we lose our personality and uniqueness. A number of practical guidelines are summarized for growing into personal uniqueness and for finding the way back to the unconditional love of God when we are overcome by feelings of a lost sense of identity. Finally our hope is in the promise that God is the keeper of our secret name, the name which expresses each person uniquely — the revelation of that name and identity is an eternal secret between the Maker and each named person.

Questions

1. If it is not true that coming to faith means we lose our uniqueness and identity, why do so many people have that impression?
2. What do you think of the claim that it is by asserting ourselves that we become who we really are?
3. How should we understand it when the Bible calls us simultaneously to become ourselves and to deny ourselves?

Bible Readings

Genesis 1–3; 4:7; Exodus 39:8–18; Proverbs 27:17, 28; 3:8,9, 4:7; Daniel 1; Luke 8:24; 15:11–32; 19:5; John 10; 15:4; Romans 7:7–17; 8:15; Ephesians 4:14–16; 5:18; 6:12; Colossians 3:1–3,9,12; 1 Jn. 5:1; Revelation 2:17.

For Further Reading

Calvin, J. *Institutes*, Vol II (Florida: MacDill, MacDonald Publishing Company)

Harris, T.A. *I'm OK — you're OK* (Harper and Row, 1973)

Hesse, H. *Steppenwolf* (Houghton on Mifflin: Penguin, 1990)

Lasch, C. *The Culture of Narcissism* (Abacus, 1980)

Nouwen, H.J.M. *The return of the Prodigal Son* (Darton, Longman and Todd, 1992)

Pascal, B. *Pensées* (Penguin Classics, 1966)

Rhinehart,L. *Adventures of Wim* (Grafton Books, 1986)

Schaeffer, F.A. 'How then should we live', *The Complete Works of Francis A. Schaeffer, Vol. 5: A Christian View of the West* (Carlisle: Paternoster, 1995)

Trobisch, W. *Love yourself* (Editions Trobisch)

Vitz, P.C. *Psychology as Religion* (Carlisle: Paternoster, 1995)